The Sinopedia Series

CHINA'S ECONOMY

The Sinopedia Series

CHINA'S ECONOMY

WU LI
SUI FUMIN

Australia • Brazil • Japan • Korea • Mexico • Singapore • Spain • United Kingdom • United States

China's Economy
Wu Li and Sui Fumin

Publishing Director:
Paul Tan

Editorial Manager:
Yang Liping

Associate Development Editor:
Joe Ng

Associate Development Editor:
Tanmayee Bhatwadekar

Senior Product Director:
Janet Lim

Product Managers:
Kevin Joo
Lee Hong Tan

Assistant Publishing Manager:
Pauline Lim

Production Executive:
Cindy Chai

Translator:
David Gu

Copy Editor:
Deborah Tham

Cover Designer:
Ong Lay Keng

Compositor:
Integra Software Services,
Pvt. Ltd.

© 2011 Cengage Learning Asia Pte Ltd
Original Chinese edition © 2010 China Intercontinental Press

For permission to use material from this
text or product, submit all requests online at
www.cengageasia.com/permissions
Further permissions questions can be emailed to
asia.permissionrequest@cengage.com

ISBN-13: 978-981-4319-74-4

ISBN-10: 981-4319-74-0

Cengage Learning Asia Pte Ltd
5 Shenton Way #01-01
UIC Building
Singapore 068808

Cengage Learning is a leading provider of customized learning solutions with office locations around the globe, including Singapore, the United Kingdom, Australia, Mexico, Brazil, and Japan. Locate your local office at: **www.cengage.com/global**

Cengage Learning products are represented in Canada by Nelson Education, Ltd.

For product information, visit **www.cengageasia.com**

Printed in Singapore
1 2 3 4 5 12 11 10

Table of Contents

Preface

After more than 30 years of sustained rapid development since the implementation of the reform and opening-up policy in 1978, China has achieved stunning and eye-catching economic growth. She is now the world's third largest economy with her staple industrial and agricultural products ranked at the top worldwide. China's international status is also rising by the day. From the "Clay-footed Giant" and "Sleeping Lion in the East" in the eighteenth century to the "Soaring Dragon" in the twenty-first century, China has traveled a long road of economic development. Nevertheless, for most foreigners, China still appears unusual, mysterious, and complex.

In the thirteenth century, when Marco Polo was touring different parts of China, he saw prosperity and fortune, and he conveyed his wonder to his fellow Westerners. Since then, Westerners have viewed this mysterious nation in the East with curiosity. After the Western powers opened up agrarian China with their mighty gunships and cannons in the mid-nineteenth century, they saw an ancient empire fraught with acute social conflicts. On the one hand was the extreme luxury and flagrant greed of the emperor and the ruling class, on

China's rapidly developing economy has become a driving force of the global economy.

the other hand was common people living in abject poverty and misery. This was aptly described in a famous verse by Du Fu, a poet from the Tang Dynasty (618–907),

> *Meat and wine go to waste behind the vermillion gates of the wealthy merchants,*
> *while wretched skeletons lie frozen on the streets.*

This tottering empire was characterized by a Confucian culture completely alien to the Westerners. However, it succumbed easily under the heavy pressure of the Western powers. In the ensuing century, the agony of war plagued China endlessly.

It was not until the mid-twentieth century, with the founding of the People's Republic of China in 1949, that China finally achieved her own independence. Since then, she has started the journey of economic development. A planned economic system became a reasonable choice in light of the historical situation

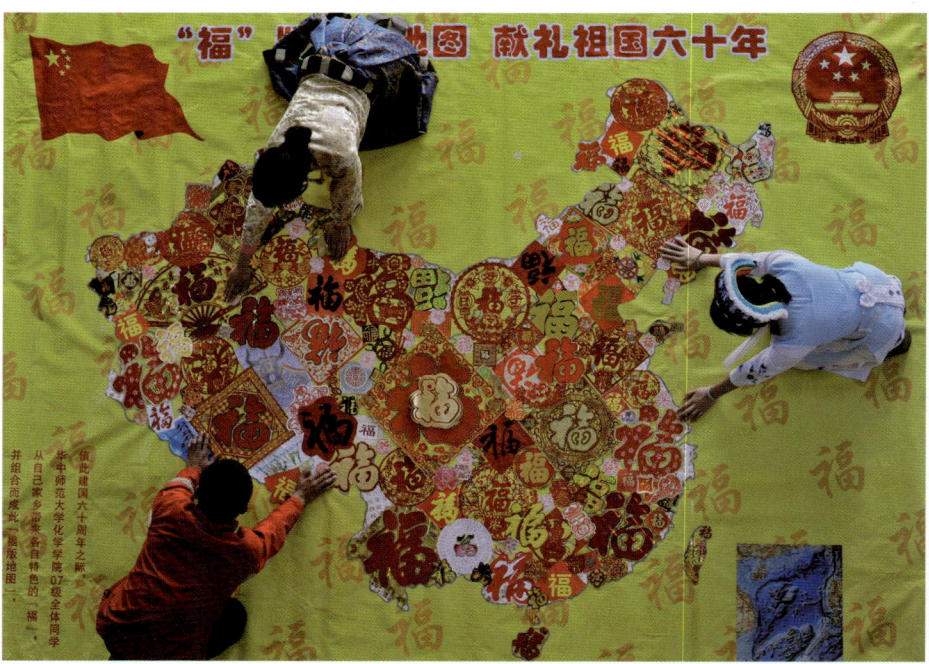

Students of different ethnic groups from Huazhong Normal University creating a map of China from 200 pieces of embroideries, paper cuttings, and other artworks collected from their hometowns during the Spring Festival. The map was dedicated to the 60th anniversary of the founding of the People's Republic of China.

of the 1950s; China followed closely the Soviet Union's traditional socialist economic model.

At the end of the 1970s, China set out on a path of reform and opening up under the leadership of Deng Xiaoping. This journey led to over 30 years of rapid development with an annual average economic growth rate close to 10%, resulting in a stable and harmonious society and a contented life for her people. China gradually became an important driving force behind the global economic growth. However, as China's economic status rose, so did misunderstanding and distortion in the international community. Of course, some scholars maintain that China's economic development has created a "China model" and that such a model deserves respect from the people around the world.

During the Asian financial crisis in 1997, China portrayed herself as a responsible great power. Today, in the face of the deepening global financial crisis and its severe aftermaths, China has once again assumed the role of a capable and responsible great power.

The world pays attention to the voice of China, who declares that she will first of all properly manage her own affairs instead of interfering in the affairs of other nations. All nations must strengthen coordination in macroeconomic policies; establish a fair, impartial, tolerant, and orderly new international financial order; improve the representation and right of speech of developing countries within international financial institutions; promote and improve international financial monitoring mechanisms; improve the global currency system, construct a sound regulatory and control mechanism for the issuance of a reserve currency; oppose protectionism in various forms; and maintain an open and free environment for trade and investment. The international community should continue to focus their attention on development issues, and further support and assist the developing countries.

The world has also noticed China's firm actions, such as providing US$10 billion in credit to support and assist the member countries of Shanghai Cooperation Organization in coping with the impact of the global financial crisis; encouraging relevant parties to reach a consensus on establishing a US$120 billion foreign exchange reserve pool for Asia by the end of 2009; actively participating in the trade and finance plans of the international finance companies and supporting an increased quota to the International Monetary Fund (IMF); and dispatching a series of trade and investment promotion groups to Europe, the United States, and member countries of the Shanghai Cooperation Organization.

The world cannot help but focus its attention on China due to her growing economic strength. Why does China hold the world's attention? Will China's economy continue to grow rapidly or will it collapse? What is the Chinese economy's secret of success? Will China become a wealthy, harmonious, and democratic nation? What contributions will China make to the global economy? This book will set out to provide brief answers to all these important questions.

Chapter 1

China's Economic Geography

A prerequisite of understanding China's economy is to first understand her economic geography. Besides providing the conditions and foundation for China's economic development, her economic geography also constrains the development of China's economy. The statistical data in this chapter is mostly sourced from the China National Bureau of Statistics, *Statistical Bulletin of the People's Republic of China* (PRC) on the 2008 National Economic and Social Development (in Chinese), February 26, 2009.

Geography

China is situated in the eastern part of the Asian continent, along the western coast of the Pacific Ocean. The outline of her territory looks like a crowing rooster with its head facing east and its tail pointing west. China has a land area of approximately 9.6 million square kilometers, which makes her the third largest country in the world after Russia and Canada. Both the north–south and east–west axes of the country exceed 5,000 kilometers. A flight from Harbin in the northeast to Haikou in southern China lasts over six hours; and a flight from Changchun in the northeast to Urumqi in the westernmost part of China takes about seven hours.

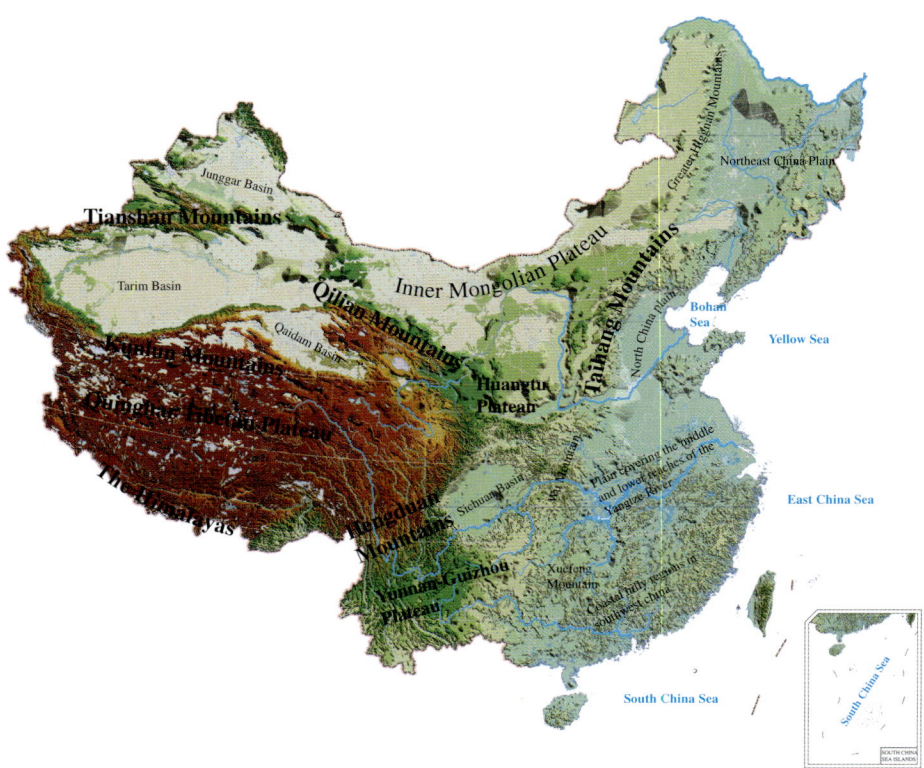

The relief map of China.

China's borders are 22,800 kilometers long and are shared with North Korea in the east and Mongolia in the north. It borders Russia in the northeast and Kazakhstan, Kyrgyzstan, and Tajikistan in the northwest. The border is shared with Afghanistan, Pakistan, India, Nepal, and Bhutan in the west and southwest, and is contiguous with Myanmar, Laos, and Vietnam in the south. The seas separate China from South Korea, Japan, the Philippines, Brunei, Malaysia, and Indonesia in the east and southeast.

China's territorial seas cover an area of 4.73 million square kilometers and her continental coastline is 18,000 kilometers long. The eastern and southern part of the Chinese mainland is surrounded by the Bohai Sea, the Yellow Sea, the East China Sea, and the South China Sea. The Bohai Sea is an inland sea of China, while the Yellow Sea, the East China Sea and the South China Sea are adjacent to the Pacific Ocean.

China is a mountainous country with about two-thirds of her landmass made up of mountainous regions (e.g., mountains, hills, and plateau), while the basins and plains only account for the remaining one-third. The overall layout of China's terrain is characterized by a higher western section and a lower eastern section, which roughly resembles a "staircase." The highest "stair" is the Qinghai-Tibet Plateau, with an average elevation of 4,000 meters above sea level, also known as the "Roof of the World." The second "stair" stretches from the Qinghai-Tibet Plateau to the north and east, consisting of the Inner Mongolia Plateau, Loess Plateau, Yungui Plateau, Tarim Basin, Junggar Basin, and Sichuan Basin, with an average elevation of 1,000–2,000 meters above sea level. The third "stair" stretches from the Greater Khingan Mountains, Taihang Mountains, Wushan Mountains, and Xuefeng Mountain eastward to the coastline, which mostly consists of plains at a sea elevation of 200 meters and below, occasionally interrupted by small hills with elevations of 1,000 meters and below. The last "stair" is the continental shelf neritic zone, with an average water depth of less than 200 meters.

China has many rivers; more than 1,500 of these rivers have drainage areas larger than 1,000 square kilometers. The Yangtze River, with a total length of 6,300 kilometers, is the longest in China, making it the third longest river in the world after the Nile River in Africa and the Amazon River in South America. The Yellow River is the second longest river in China, with a total length of 5,464 kilometers. The Yangtze River Basin and Yellow River Basin are both called "Cradles of the Chinese Civilization." Most areas in China are located inside the North Temperate Zone, which features mild weather and distinct seasonal variations, making it an ideal place for human habitation.

Natural Resources

By the end of 2008, there were 121,716,000 hectares of arable land in China. The Northeast China Plain, North China Plain, Middle-Lower Yangtze Plain, Zhujiang (Pearl River) Delta, and Sichuan Basin have the highest concentration of arable land. The Northeast Plain is the largest plain in China; it covers an area of over 350,000 square kilometers. It consists mostly of fertile black earth, and produces abundant harvests of wheat, paddy, maize, soybean, sorghum, flax, and beet. The North China Plain features mostly brown soil, with deep soil layers; suitable crops include wheat, maize, grain, and cotton. The plains of the middle and lower reaches of the Yangtze River feature low and flat terrain densely dotted with rivers and lakes, and is China's most productive area of paddy and freshwater fish, famously known as "The Land of Fish and Paddy," as well as producing abundant amounts of tea leaves and silk. The

Sichuan Basin has a warm and wet climate and features purple soil; the crops can grow for all four seasons throughout the year and it produces harvests of paddy, rape, and sugar cane, earning it the nickname of "The Land of Abundance." The Zhujiang Delta produces paddy in great quantities, and reaps two to three harvests each year.

China's forested area covers about 174,910,000 hectares and the grasslands occupy about 400 million hectares. Natural grasslands can be found throughout the country, divided by administrative provinces. The Tibet Autonomous Region has the largest area of grasslands, approximately 70,846,800 hectares in the whole region, accounting for 21.4% of the country's total. This is followed by the Inner Mongolia Autonomous Region, Xinjiang Uyghur Autonomous Region, and Qinghai Province where the grassland area accounts for 64.65% of the country's total. Other provinces or regions with 10 million hectares or more of grassland include Sichuan, Gansu, and Yunnan. The Inner Mongolia Autonomous Region has the largest cultivated grassland and semi-cultivated grassland in China, boasting 4,433,400 hectares of artificial grassland area; other provinces and regions with one million hectares or more of the cultivated and semi-artificial grasslands include (in descending order) Sichuan Province, Xinjiang Uygur Autonomous Region, Qinghai Province, and Gansu Province. Owing to the rich grassland resources, the provinces (or regions) of Inner Mongolia, Gansu, Xinjiang, and Qinghai also have a competitive advantage in the industry of husbandry development. While the absolute quantity of China's arable land, forest, and grassland area occupies leading positions in the world, its per capita quantity is nonetheless relatively small. China's per capita arable land is only one-fourth of the world's average per capita value while her per capita forest reserve is only one-eighth of the world's average per capita reserve.

Rivers and lakes make up China's main sources of fresh water. The total volume of China's water resources is 2.7127 trillion cubic meters, averaging about 2,000 cubic meters per capita. With the low usage of water resources and low per capita volume, China is ranked globally at 121st for per capita water resources. She is also included among 13 countries with low per capita water resources consumption. Meanwhile, the distribution of water resources is also extremely unbalanced, with abundant supply in the south and relative scarcity in the north. This is exemplified by regular floods in the south and frequent droughts in the north. China's hydraulic resource reserves are 676 million kilowatts, making her the top in the world. The Yangtze River water system contains the most reserves, followed by the Brahmaputra River water system. However, its distribution is also extremely unbalanced, with the reserves being mostly concentrated in the inner region of southwest China.

Existing proven mineral resource reserves in China account for about 12% of the world's reserves, making her the world's third largest holder of mineral resources (after the United States and Russia). However, owing to her large population, China's per capita mineral resources is only 58% of the world's average level, and the per capita amount for 45 mineral resources is lower than half of the world's average. There are altogether 171 varieties of proven mineral resources in China, of which the reserves of 158 mineral resources met the minimum levels required for mining, such as 10 energy carriers, 41 non-ferrous metals, eight precious metals, five ferrous metals, 91 non-metals as well as three liquid and gaseous mineral resources. China ranks top in the world for her reserves of 12 mineral resources, such as vanadium, titanium, tantalum, boron, antimony, tungsten, graphite, sodium sulfate, barite, magnesium, and gypsum. Her reserves of coal, iron, lead, zinc, copper, silver, mercury, tin, nickel, apatite, and asbestos all surpass the leading countries in the world. China's available coal reserves exceed 1 trillion tons, most of which are found in the northern part of the country, especially so for Shanxi Province and Inner Mongolia Autonomous Region. Her iron ore reserves reach 45.7 billion tons, and are mainly distributed in the northeastern, eastern, and southwestern parts of China. China also has an extremely abundant supply of petroleum, natural gas, oil shale, phosphorous, sulfur, and other mineral resources. Petroleum is mainly deposited in the northwestern regions, followed by the northeastern and northern China as well as the continental shelf in the eastern coastal areas.

Administrative and Economic Divisions

Currently, there are 34 provincial-level administrative regions in mainland China; 23 provinces, five autonomous regions, four municipalities directly under the administration of the central government, and two special administrative regions (SARs). In terms of historical usage and established practice, all provincial-level administrative regions have their own abbreviated names. The seat of the provincial-level government is called the provincial capital (the capital city); Beijing is the capital of the country, where the central government is located. Township is the most basic administrative unit in China. Autonomous regions, autonomous prefectures, and autonomous counties are self-governed areas where they are predominantly inhabited by the ethnic minorities. All these areas are integral to China's sovereignty.

Historically, Hong Kong and Macau were once separated from mainland China. The Chinese government regained the exercise of its sovereignty over

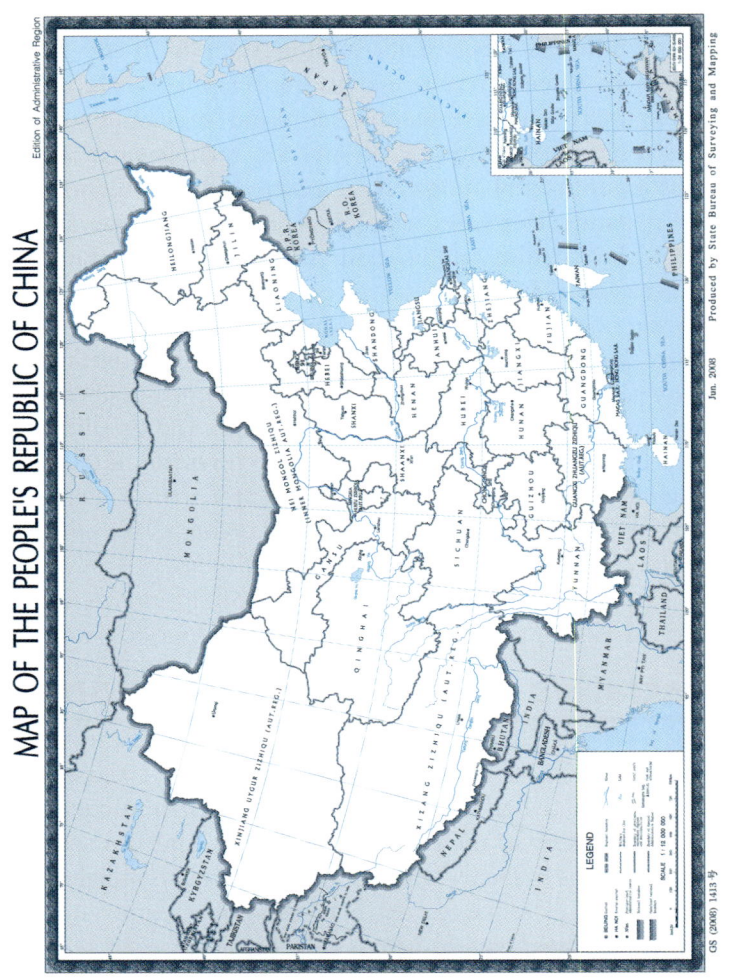

Hong Kong on July 1, 1997, and set up a local government for the Hong Kong SAR. She also regained the exercise of sovereignty over Macau and set up a local government for the Macau SAR on December 20, 1999. Historically, Taiwan is also considered a part of China.

According to the second National Economic Census in 2008, mainland China is divided into three main economic regions: the Eastern Region, the Central Region, and the Western Region. The Eastern Region includes Beijing, Tianjin, Hebei, Liaoning, Shanghai, Jiangsu, Zhejiang, Fujian, Shandong, Guangdong, and Hainan; the Central Region includes Shanxi, Jilin, Heilongjiang, Anhui, Jiangxi, Henan, Hubei, and Hunan; the Western Region includes Inner Mongolia, Guangxi, Chongqing, Sichuan, Guizhou, Yunnan, Tibet, Shaanxi, Gansu, Qinghai, Ningxia, and Xinjiang.

The three main economic regions can be further subdivided into the Eastern Region, Central Region, Western Region and Northeast Region. The Eastern Region includes 10 provinces and municipalities: Beijing, Tianjin, Hebei, Shanghai, Jiangsu, Zhejiang, Fujian, Shandong, Guangdong, and Hainan; the Central Region includes six provinces: Shanxi, Anhui, Jiangxi, Henan, Hubei, and Hunan; the Western Region includes 12 provinces, regions, and municipalities: Inner Mongolia, Guangxi, Chongqing, Sichuan, Guizhou, Yunnan, Tibet, Shaanxi, Gansu, Qinghai, Ningxia, and Xinjiang; the Northeastern Region includes three provinces: Liaoning, Jilin, and Heilongjiang.

Population

China has the largest population among all countries in the world. In 2008, the total population of mainland China was approximately 1,328,020,000. The population of the Hong Kong SAR was approximately 6,930,000, the population of the Macau SAR was about 530,000, and that of Taiwan was approximately 23 million. China has one of the highest levels of population density in the world, with her average population density at 134 people per square kilometers. However, China's population is not evenly distributed: the population in the eastern coastal regions is dense, with over 400 people per square kilometers; whereas in the central region, there are more than 200 people per square kilometers; the population in the western plateau region is scarce, with less than 10 people per square kilometers.

Since the implementation of the 1978 reform and opening-up policy, and the subsequent enforcement of the family planning policy, China's birth rate decreased steadily. China's proportion of the world's population has dropped from 22.2% in 1980 to 20.1% in 2007; it has completed the transformation from a traditional model of "high birth rate, low mortality rate, and high natu-

The rapidly growing population is the most challenging issue that China faces currently.

ral growth" to the contemporary model of "low birth rate, low mortality rate, and low natural growth." With improvements in living standards and better public health care, the overall health of China's population has shown significant improvements. The infant mortality rate has progressively dropped while life expectancy has increased dramatically. The overall educational level of the population has also improved significantly and China's urban population has reached 45.7% of her total population.

Population composition of China in 2008						
Gender (%)		Urban/Rural (%)		Age (%)		
Male	Female	Urban	Rural	≤ 14	15–59	≥ 60
51.5	48.5	45.7	54.3	19.0	69.0	12.0

Source: Statistical Bulletin of China's Economic and Social Development in 2008, China National Bureau of Statistics.

Urban Cities

With the acceleration of China's industrialization, modernization, and urbanization, both the number and scale of cities in China have expanded continuously. At the end of 2007, there were 655 cities in China, of which 287 were prefectural level and above. There were 36 municipal districts (excluding municipal counties) with populations exceeding two million, and 83 cities with a population of one to two million. The scale of cities is also expanding continually. The nationwide land area of the administrative area of prefectural level and above cities (excluding municipal counties) was 622,000 square kilometers. The development of small townships shows a new trend with the number of small townships growing rapidly. At the end of 2008, China had an urban population of 607 million; the level of urbanization reached 45.68%, an increase of 35 percentage points compared to 1949.

At the end of 2007, the regional distribution of China's cities was as follows:

- North China (77);
- Northeast China (90);
- East China (188);
- South China (177);
- Southwest China (65);
- Northwest China (60);
- Taiwan (39); and
- Hong Kong and Macau (2).

The distribution of mainland Chinese cities by province was as follows:

- Shandong Province (48);
- Guangdong Province (44);
- Jiangsu Province (40);
- Henan Province (39);
- Hubei Province (36);
- Zhejiang Province (33);
- Hebei Province (33);
- Sichuan Province (32);
- Liaoning Province (31);
- Heilongjiang Province (31);
- Hunan Province (29);
- Jilin Province (28);
- Fujian Province (23);
- Anhui Province (22);
- Shanxi Province (22);

In recent years, urbanization has increased rapidly and is expected to accelerate further in the near future.

- Jiangxi Province (21);
- Guangxi Zhuang Autonomous Region (21);
- Xinjiang Uygur Autonomous Region (21);
- Inner Mongolian Autonomous Region (20);
- Yunnan Province (17);
- Gansu Province (16);
- Shaanxi Province (13);
- Guizhou Province (13);
- Hainan Province (8);
- Ningxia Hui Autonomous Region (7);
- Qinghai Province (3); and
- Tibet Autonomous Region (2).

Transportation

China's standards of transportation infrastructure improved significantly along with her economic development. In 2008, China had 80,000 kilometers of railway in operation, 3,730,000 kilometers of roads, 123,000 kilometers of navigable inland river routes, and 2,462,000 kilometers of civil aviation routes. National passenger volume reached 28.7 billion persons, passenger turnover volume hit 2,319.7 billion persons, while cargo transport volume reached 25.9 billion tons, and cargo turnover volume exceeded 11 trillion ton-kilometers. There were 18,437 railway locomotives, 51 million private automobiles, while the number of private transport ships reached 184,190 vessels and the cargo turnover of major ports along the coastline was about 4.3 billion tons.

Toward the end of 2007, China had completed and put into operation 12 state highway trunk lines (also known as the "5 Vertical Axes and 7 Horizontal Axes" highways). By 2010, China's highway network will have basically taken shape, and the technical grade of both the national and provincial trunk line highways will experience further improvements. In 2010, the eight inter-province highways for the development of the Western Region should be completed. During the construction of the highway networks, the central government placed strong emphasis on the 14 routes of the "Five Spokes, Two Vertical Axes, and Seven Horizontal Axes" Plan,[1] which is targeted for completion by 2010.

By 2010, coastal ports will be developed in an organized manner. The deployment of large specialized wharfs for transporting coal, crude oil, liquefied natural gas, iron ore, and containers will start to take shape. Key emphasis will be placed on the construction of the three international shipping centers in Shanghai, Tianjin, and Dalian.

Environment

Owing to its large population and relatively low standard of economic development, China has to face the challenge of protecting her environment and ecology throughout the development process. In 1972, China was a delegate at the first United Nations Conference on the Human Environment (UNCHE). Nevertheless, with the rapid development of China's economy, efforts in environmental regulation have been doubled every year.

In 2007, China made breakthroughs in energy conservation and emissions cuts: both her chemical oxygen demand (COD) and discharge of sulfur dioxide decreased. In 2008, the country reached an afforested area of 4.77 million hectares, the number of nature reserves climbed to 2,538, of

---

[1]"Five Spokes": Beijing–Shanghai, Beijing–Fuzhou, Beijing–Hong Kong & Macau, Beijing–Kunming, Beijing–Harbin; "Two Vertical Axes": Shenyang–Haikou, Baotou–Maoming; "Seven Horizontal Axes": Qingdao–Yinchuan, Nanjing–Luoyang, Shanghai–Xi'an, Shanghai–Chongqing, Shanghai–Kunming, Fuzhou–Yinchuan, Guangzhou–Kunming.

which 303 were state-level nature reserves. Natural wetlands enjoyed improved protection and her ecology and environment experienced gradual restoration and improvement. The treatment of water and soil loss problems achieved new breakthroughs. China has also become extremely active in international cooperation and exchange regarding environmental protection, and has signed agreements on environmental cooperation with a number of countries.

Before the World Climate Conference convened in Copenhagen during December 7–18, 2009, the Chinese government announced her goal of reducing greenhouse emissions by 40 to 45% of carbon dioxide emission per gross domestic product (GDP) in 2020, based on the measured levels in 2005. This pledge far exceeded the promises made by other major emitters in the world. This not only validates the notion that the Chinese government is willing to make tireless efforts for the welfare of her people, but she also maintains a high sense of responsibility for humankind. Henceforth, China is participating in global environmental affairs with a more open attitude and pragmatic spirit of cooperation.

China is aware of the importance of protecting the environment after having experienced the harmful effects of industrialization. This picture shows the beautiful Shenyang city against a clear blue sky, a result of effective measures taken to protect the environment.

Chapter 2

China's Economy: History and Development

Modern China's economic development has been exceptional: the current achievements represent the unyielding pursuit of industrialization and modernization by the Chinese people. After more than 60 years of ups and downs, the Chinese people are now more mature, rational, and confident in blazing their own paths. Along the way, a socialist economy with Chinese characteristics was formed.

The Heavy Capitalization and Prioritized Development of Heavy Industries (1949–1978)

On October 1, 1949, the People's Republic of China was founded, thus putting an end to social mayhem that had plagued China for the past 100 years. A powerful and efficient government was established, hence providing a safeguard for economic development. Nevertheless, it was still necessary to develop the economy.

At that time, the new government was facing a quandary. In 1949, China's average grain production was only 71 kilograms per *mu* (1 *mu* ≈ 667 square meters), 4 kilograms lower than the world's average. Her labor productivity level was relatively low and industrial production lagged far behind other nations. Her annual production of iron and steel was at 410,000 tons while crude oil production was at 120,000 tons.

For the first time after 1,000 years, the nationwide land reform (1949–1953) made it possible for Chinese farmers to become land owners and this greatly aroused their enthusiasm for production. This picture shows poor farmers in Northeast China planting signs to claim their farmland.

After the founding of the People's Republic of China in 1949, the primary task of the government was to restore and develop the national economy. The overall economic guideline adopted by the government was "to place equal emphasis on public and private interests, in order to benefit workers and enterprises; to build urban and rural partnerships, and encourage internal and external exchanges." Through a series of effective economic policies, the government unified the currency and financial systems, thus achieving a balance between China's income and expenditure, and successfully controlled high inflation that had troubled the nation for 13 years. At the same time, the government exerted its authority on resource allocation and sorted out central–local government relations. After implementing a series of policies and measures aimed at reforming and rejuvenating the economy, the government managed to restart industrial production, increase employment opportunities, thus achieving social stability.

In the rural areas, the government adopted sweeping land reforms, turning the concept of "a plot of land for every farmer" into a reality. This policy brought significant changes to the ownership structure of farmland and other means of production in China's rural areas. The previous landlord economy was replaced with one of small-scale farming by individual owners with each household representing a basic economic unit.

In the cities, the government eliminated the economic privileges of the imperialists, confiscated bureaucratic capital, and established a state-owned economy. Through the government's regulation and management, it incorporated the private economy into a neo-democratic economic system.

By 1952, China had fulfilled the task of restoring the postwar national economy within three years. The output of her nationwide industrial and agricultural staple products exceeded the pre-1949 historical levels, while the Chinese people's living standards showed marked improvement.

FYI
FOR YOUR
INFORMATION

THE HUMBLE BEGINNING OF CHINA'S ECONOMY

In the modern era, owing to her under-industrialization, China was subjected to humiliation and pressure from the Western powers. Recurring domestic troubles and foreign invasions plunged the country into misery and suffering; this caused China's international standing to plummet to a historical low. From 1840 to 1940, China experienced 12 major wars and revolutions, in which six were wars against foreign invasions (the First Opium War, the Second Opium War, the Sino-French War, the Sino-Japanese War of 1894–1895, the Eight-Power Allied Forces War of Aggression against China, and the War of Resistance against Japan), and six were civil wars (the Taiping Heavenly Kingdom Movement, the Boxers Uprising, the Revolution of 1911, the Second Revolution, the Northern Expedition War, the Central Plains' War, the Agrarian Revolutionary War, and the War of Liberation). Imperialist invasions, feudalism's oppression and the direct and indirect economic losses brought about by the above-mentioned wars slowed down China's economic development and held back her industrialization.

At the founding of the People's Republic of China in 1949, China's per capita national income was only RMB66.10. From 1840 to 1949, the annual average GDP growth was less than 1%. In 1949, out of the total gross industrial and agricultural output, agriculture took up 70% while industries accounted for 30%, while the gross output of heavy industries was only 7.9% of the gross agricultural output. At that time, China was viewed as an impoverished and backward agricultural nation.

Meanwhile, between 1820 and 1950, the world economy achieved unprecedented progress. The world's GDP increased 7.68-fold and per capita GDP increased 3.17-fold. The United State's per capita GDP increased 7.61-fold, western Europe's per capita GDP increased 3.73-fold and Japan's per capita GDP increased 2.88-fold. However, China's per capita GDP fell. According to the results of a study by British economist Angus Maddison, China's GDP fell from 90% of the world's average GDP in 1820 to 21% of the world's average GDP in 1950. The percentage of China's contribution to global GDP also dropped from 33.3% to 4.5%.

While restoring and developing the economy, China's external environment also underwent changes. In June 1950, the Korean War broke out. In order to safeguard the security of the nation and protect the industries in Northeast China from external threats, China dispatched a volunteer army across the Korean border. The war lasted for three years, until an armistice agreement was signed in Panmunjom, North Korea, in July 1953. China had to give equal emphasis on restoring her economy and yet ensure that there were enough supplies to keep the troops going. The Chinese people had to made great sacrifices to ensure sufficient war supplies while simultaneously building up the economy. According to estimates made by the authors of *The Cambridge History of China,* war expenses incurred during the war by China reached US$10 billion. In addition, the politics of the Cold War further caused a negative impact on China's economic growth.

In 1949, China tried to improve her relationship with the Western powers in order to create a conducive environment for developing her economy. However, due to the political context of the Cold War, China had no choice but to fall in line with the socialist camp headed by the Soviet Union.

Joining the socialist camp not only provided China with allies and partners within the international community, but also supplied empirical experience and aid supplies for economic development. Soviet Union's well-planned economy had achieved great successes in the 1930s and laid the foundation for the country's victory in the Second World War. She also scored significant achievements in her post-war economic recovery, thereby elevating her economic strength and international status, earning worldwide respect. On the other hand, from China's upper echelon of leaders down to her common people, everyone was anxious to achieve the same rapid industrialization and international standing. The people had hoped to accelerate economic development within a peaceful and stable domestic and international environment, in order to improve China's then-backward conditions.

To follow the path of socialist industrialization, which places a high priority on the development of heavy industries, China selected an economic model that incorporates a single sector of public ownership and central planning. The backward state of China's heavy industries at that time was not only a bottleneck to economic development, but also created a serious hurdle to the construction of a strong national defense. Without developed heavy industries, there was no safeguard for China's national security, and she would face attacks from foreign nations; a bitter experience endured by the Chinese people for more than 100 years. In the early 1950s, the Chinese leadership decided to make the development of heavy industries and industrialization efforts a key priority. At a time of extreme shortage of capital, China had to depend on the "visible hand" of the government to allocate resources in order to achieve this key goal. This was the only way to allocate limited resources in order to achieve maximum utilization. Focusing on industrial construction within a planned economy, the government's allocation of products such as grain, cotton, steel, coal, cement, power, and so on, was advantageous under the following conditions:

- when market adjustment could not effectively increase supply in the short term and demand flexibility was too small;
- when there was an acute shortage of capital and a limited surplus in agricultural products; and
- when the supply and consumption structure were both very simple.

As a result, from 1953, China began her socialist transition toward a single sector of public ownership and a planned economy for the purpose of carrying out large-scale economic growth.

During the First Five-Year Plan (1953–1957), China kicked off a large-scale economic plan, which focused on introducing advanced technologies from the Soviet Union. The successful launch and completion of some major projects transformed the poor and desolate outlook of China's industrial landscape—the most prominent evidence was the 156 large projects constructed with aid from the Soviet Union. The industrial departments and production capacity developed by these projects not only filled up many gaps in the economy, but also improved the productivity of weaker sectors. This rapidly enhanced the technical standards of China's industrial development, thus enabling her to establish a strong industrial foundation.

FYI
FOR YOUR
INFORMATION

FIVE-YEAR PLANS

As part of China's national economic plan, the main aims of a Five-Year Plan were to build key national infrastructure, improve the overall productivity of the industries, and enhance relationships between the state and people of the national economy. Thus, the targets and directions for the development and growth of the economy can be met. Since the founding of the People's Republic of China in 1949 (excluding the period between 1963 and 1965, which was a period of adjustment for the national economy), between 1953 and 2005, China implemented 10 Five-Year Plans. Presently, China is implementing her 11th Five-Year Plan (2006–2010), and the term has since been renamed to Five-Year Guidelines.

Large-scale industrial construction requires vast amounts of capital, raw material, and grain, but all these were lacking in China. During the Cold War, apart from the very limited capital assistance from the Soviet Union, the only way to build capital reserves was to rely on domestic accumulation, with this main responsibility placed on the relatively backward agricultural sector. The adoption of agricultural cooperatives was seen at that time as a method to enhance agricultural production standards and fully utilize labor resources. As a result, the government accelerated the pace of consolidating farms into cooperatives. By the end of 1956, peasants participating in agricultural cooperatives accounted for 96.3% of the total farming households. Within a short span of four years, the socialist transformation of agriculture was successfully completed.

Through agricultural cooperatives, the government transformed the farming household's private ownership of the means of production into collective ownership; the production and operating methods of agriculture also shifted from each individual household to a joint collective. Due to excessive and urgent demands, inefficient work procedures, rapid changes in ownership, and too similar strategies in the later stages of the cooperative period, some cooperatives violated the principles of self-sacrifice and mutual benefits. This resulted in the collective economy failing to show its supposed superior advantages. Meanwhile, the government also deprived the farmers of their rights to independently dispose of their surplus products through the state monopoly of purchase and sales of main agricultural products and non-staple foodstuff products.

156 PROJECTS AND CHINA'S INDUSTRIAL DISTRIBUTION

Out of the 156 projects receiving aid from the Soviet Union during the First Five-Year Plan, 150 projects were started. This included 44 enterprises in the military industry (12 were in the aviation industry, 10 in the electronics industry, 16 in the weapons industry, two in the aerospace industry, and four in the shipping industry); 20 enterprises in the metallurgy industry (seven were in the iron and steel industry and 13 in the non-ferrous industry); seven enterprises in the chemical industry; 24 enterprises in mechanical processing; 52 enterprises in the energy industry (25 were in coal and power generation industries, and two in the petroleum industry); and three enterprises categorized under both the light industry and pharmaceutical industry. The aim of these projects was to build up vital and comprehensive industrial and national defense industries for China, so as to lay down the basic foundations of her industrialization.

The industrial construction of the First Five-Year Plan centered on 156 projects that enabled China's industrial technical standards to rapidly improve. From lagging behind developed industrial nations in 1949, China advanced her position to reach the prevailing standard by the 1950s. By 1957, China had progressively built up eight major industrial zones centered in large and mid-sized cities: the Northeast Industrial Hub around Shenyang and Anshan; the North China Industrial Hub around Beijing, Tianjin, and Tangshan; the Shanxi Industrial Hub around Taiyuan; the Hubei Industrial Hub around Wuhan; the Zheng-Luo-Bian Industrial Hub around Zhengzhou; the Shaanxi Industrial Hub around Xi'an; the Gansu Industrial Hub around Lanzhou; and the South Sichuan Industrial Hub around Chongqing.

The First Five-Year Plan brought fundamental changes to China's unbalanced industrial conditions, as 70% of her industries and industrial cities were concentrated in the eastern coastal regions before 1949.

The transformation of the handicrafts industry into cooperatives was also very successful. In 1953, only 3.9% of people were working in handicraft cooperatives. But the figure rose to 26.9% in 1955 and achieved 91.7% the following year.

The transformation of private industry and trade began in 1949. Prior to 1952, it was primarily carried out through the methods of "making orders for processing" and "unified purchase and sale." After 1953, "public–private joint management" was enforced for single enterprises, and by the later half of 1955, the practice of "public–private joint management" had spread throughout the whole industry. The government completed the socialist transformation through the equitable purchase approach of "public–private joint management" toward the whole industry. The government only allowed owners of private enterprises to collect fixed interest while forcing them to hand over the enterprises' operating and management rights. By the end of 1956, the private economy had significantly disappeared, the individual economy had become negligible, and the ownership structure in China essentially consisted of the state-owned enterprises (SOEs) and the collective economy.

During the period of the First Five-Year Plan, overall economic development was generally healthy, with appropriate economic ratios maintained among all industries. The industry's gross output value grew by 10.9% on average each year while the national income grew by 8.9%. American scholar John K. Fairbank praised the achievements of this period. The First Five-Year Plan played a decisive role in accelerating the growth of China's economy in the twentieth century. China's experience is considered relatively successful in light of the 2.5% per capita GDP annual growth rate among the newly independent developing countries.

However, such favorable conditions did not last long. In 1958, in view of the shortcomings of the Soviet Union's economic system, and in order to achieve faster economic development, China jumpstarted "The Great Leap Forward" and "The People's Commune" campaigns. "The Great Leap Forward" set an unrealistic industrial growth target. Owing to a severe shortage of raw materials and capital, the Chinese government tried to substitute labor for capital. In the end, steel making by indigenous methods not only failed to successfully meet targets in iron and steel making, but also wasted a tremendous amount of labor. In the countryside, the senior cooperative commune also evolved one step further into People's Communes at a "larger scale and higher level of public ownership." "The People's Commune" campaign ran contrary to the farmers' wishes and removed the concepts of self-sacrifice and mutual benefits from the cooperative economy. This not only seriously diminished farmers' initiative for production, but also gave birth to the negative practices of "Blind Guidance" and "Tendency to Boast and Exaggerate" in production and operation. Hence, there was a significant decrease in grain production and also wastage of an immense amount of grain. Combined with an outbreak of natural disasters, agricultural production dropped significantly and triggered the Great Famine between 1959 and 1961, leading to the premature deaths of vast numbers of the population. As "The Great Leap Forward" and "The People's Commune" campaigns marked a serious departure from reality, the economy sailed into dire straits. Within three years, the agricultural production dropped 22.8%, while an excessively high accumulation rate resulted in residents' living standards dropping by 4.9% each year and caused the nation's financial deficit to rise sharply.

In 1961, the economy entered a period of adjustment. The government overhauled the economic structure by reducing the scale of infrastructure

FYI
FOR YOUR INFORMATION

"THE GREAT LEAP FORWARD" AND "THE PEOPLE'S COMMUNE" CAMPAIGNS

"The Great Leap Forward" campaign refers to a nationwide radical leftist ideological campaign that was initiated by the Communist Party of China (CPC) and lasted between 1958 and 1960. Pursuing high-speed growth in production, "The Great Leap Forward" aimed at fulfilling high targets in industrial and agricultural production: it called for the output of key industrial and agricultural products to grow by not just two-fold, but several dozen times. Despite its underlying goal of improving China's backward economic and cultural situation as early as possible, there was no way that she could achieve this as the campaign neglected basic and fundamental economic concepts. "The Great Leap Forward" campaign resulted in major disturbances in the country's economic ratios and created severe economic difficulties.

The main period of "The People's Communes" campaign in China occurred between 1958 and 1984. The communes were an organization that integrated "political leadership and commune management," that is, grassroots political units (county people's committees) were integrated with the leadership institutions of collective economic organizations (commune management committees) to create a unified management for all county and commune affairs. The "People's Commune" was both a production organization and grassroots political body. In the early days of "The People's Commune," the means of production were subjected to a single communal ownership.

As for distribution, the commune implemented a system that combined wages and supply, thus eliminating private farmland and reduced each household's secondary production from communes, therefore dampening the farmers' motivation for production. This system seriously retarded the development of rural productivity. After 1962, following a series of adjustments, the majority of the People's Communes adopted a system of "three tiers of ownership with the team as the core unit." This restored and expanded private farmland and households' secondary production. However, there were still shortcomings in the form of centralized management, uniform operating methods, and egalitarianism in distribution. With the widespread adoption of the agricultural production responsibility system after 1978—represented by the household contract responsibility system in the rural areas—all the People's Communes were eventually replaced with townships

construction and increasing investments in agriculture. As a result, the economy once again returned to a healthy pace of development. After several years of adjustment, the agriculture, light industry, and heavy industries achieved relatively balanced development. Compared with 1960, agricultural output in 1965 was 42.2% higher, light industry output increased 27.5%, while heavy industries output dropped 37.2%. In addition, the state's financial situation improved, the savings rate decreased, and the living and consumption standards of urban and rural residents increased 25.7%. China's industrial construction and the science and technology sectors made considerable progress.

The Cultural Revolution began in 1966, further interrupting China's economic development progress. But China continued her process of reforming the economic system despite a decade of revolution. Although China's economy suffered great losses, she nonetheless made some progress in certain areas. Except for 1967 and 1968, gross industrial and agricultural output both achieved positive growth, and grain production maintained relatively stable growth. A slew of major achievements were made in industry, transport, infrastructure, and science and technology:

- completion of some new railways and the Nanjing Yangtze River Bridge;
- launch of major enterprises with advanced technologies;
- successful hydrogen bomb test and the launch and recovery of a man-made satellite;
- cultivation and propagation of a crossbreed rice variety.

THE CULTURAL REVOLUTION

The Proletariat Cultural Revolution (or Cultural Revolution in short) was a major political campaign that ran from 1966 to 1976. The 10 years of the Cultural Revolution are now widely regarded as the most tumultuous and disastrous period since the founding of the People's Republic of China, and therefore is generally known as the "Ten Chaotic Years" or "Ten-Year Calamity."

On June 27, 1981, the "Resolution on Certain Questions in the History of Our Party since the Founding of the People's Republic of China" was passed at the Sixth Plenary Session of the Eleventh Central Committee of the Communist Party of China. The resolution pointed out that "the 'Cultural Revolution' between May 1966 and October 1976 brought the heaviest setback and loss to the party, the nation, and the people since the founding of the Republic.... The Cultural Revolution was an internal disturbance wrongly launched by the state leadership, and was later utilized by counter-revolutionary groups to their own advantage. It was disastrous to the party, the nation, and people of all nationalities."

However, due to the chaotic situation afflicting the economic, social, and political aspects of China, industrial and agricultural production still suffered greatly. This resulted in dysfunctional development of the industrial structure, the restrained initiative of labor, little if any increase in productivity, and an acute loss in human capital. As a result, there was no improvement in people's living standards for a long period of time.

For two years after the end of the Cultural Revolution in 1976, the Chinese government tried her best to correct the mistakes made during the last 10 years and restore normal economic order. Nevertheless, China had not yet started reforming the poor efficiency of the economic system, yet it had started a new "Leap Forward," which caused further deterioration of the previously dysfunctional industrial structure and strained economic relations. The economic problems could not be effectively resolved: there were 250 million people nationwide who were still living in abject poverty.

In summary, between 1949 and 1978, China established a relatively well-developed economic system and independent industrial system with a strategy of

The Nanjing Yangtze River Bridge was completed and opened to traffic on December 29, 1968. This was an important infrastructural achievement during the Cultural Revolution. This picture shows the bridge during its 40th anniversary on December 29, 2008.

high accumulation of capital and prioritized development of heavy industry. At the same time, various acute problems also cropped up in economic development. However, these problems were difficult to resolve within the framework of a centrally planned economy and a singular public ownership system.

Reform and Opening up of China's Economy (1978–2002)

The Third Plenary Session of the 11th Central Committee of the Communist Party of China was convened at the end of 1978. This was a landmark event for China. A new group of leaders was gathered there, headed by Deng Xiaoping, who had famously said "it doesn't matter what color a cat is, as long as it hunts mice." This practical outlook ushered China onto the path of reform and opening up.

China's adoption of the reform and opening-up policy was closely linked to contemporary domestic and international events. In the 1960s, Sino-Soviet relations deteriorated. In 1971, China reclaimed its legitimate seat in the

United Nations (UN). In February 1972, China and the United States jointly announced the *Shanghai Communiqué;* officially normalizing Sino-U.S. relations. Soon afterwards, Japanese Prime Minister Tanaka Kakuei visited China, and the two countries established formal diplomatic relations. In September 1973, French President Georges Pompidou visited China, bringing Sino-French relations into a new stage. Together, these events created an international atmosphere conducive to China's reform and opening up, in sharp contrast to her previous isolationist policies. Meanwhile, the emergence of Japan and the "Four Dragons" of Asia—the four emerging industrialized nations and regions of Hong Kong, Singapore, South Korea, and Taiwan—also prompted China to review her situation. In 1978, the Chinese leadership took several trips abroad and realized how backward China's economy was. This made them realize the need and urgency to reform and open up the economy.

As the chief architect of China's reform and opening up, Deng Xiaoping addressed the Third Plenary Session in 1978: "if a party, a country or a nation does everything by following dogmas, think in an ossified manner, and follows superstitions closely, then we can never progress forward, our hopes will be extinguished, and both the party and the country is doomed.... Hence, we should allow some workers and farmers at some enterprises to enjoy a better

Deng Xiaoping was instrumental in China's reform and opening up. This picture shows a mural of the late paramount leader erected in Shenzhen, Guangdong Province.

life due to their diligence, which will result in greater achievements and higher income." His address thus unveiled a new chapter in China's endeavor of reform and opening up.

The reform of the economic system started with the policy of "delegating powers and benefits." In the cities, the reform movement progressively expanded the right of self-determination for local governments and SOEs. In the countryside, the reform movement delegated to farming households the right of self-determination for production and operation, namely transforming the practice of collective production into the "Household Contract Responsibility System"; individual households could operate their own farms independently. This reform was enthusiastically welcomed by farmers, with 93% of the nation's production teams adopting the household responsibility system by early 1983.

After overseeing the widespread implementation of the household responsibility system, the central government decided to abolish People's Communes in October 1983, and established township governments as the lowest level of

FYI
FOR YOUR INFORMATION

XIAOGANG VILLAGE IN ANHUI PROVINCE: THE FORERUNNER OF RURAL REFORM

In December 1978, 18 peasant households in Xiaogang Village, Fengyang County, Anhui Province, decided that they were no longer willing to continue starving under the system of "collective production." They gathered together and pledged to allocate individual plots of land to each household for farming. They affixed their thumbprints and wrote the following terms on their "secret agreement": "If this arrangement is leaked, the production team cadres would take full responsibility and bear all punishment, and all the commune members would raise their children until they reached the age of 18."

All signatories agreed that firstly, agricultural produce independently produced by individual households would be used for meeting the quota for state purchase. Secondly, the remaining produce would be used for the collective's consumption. Finally, any remaining produce can be used or sold at the discretion of the farmers. From then on, the system of collective production was replaced with one of production contracted to households, and a new era of rural reform began in China.

political bureacracy. At the same time, it set up villagers' committees to act as self-managing governing bodies. By spring 1985, China completed the transformation of her local political structures.

For every year between 1982 and 1986, the first official document published by the CPC Central Committee, "CPC Central Document No.1," was always related to rural economic reform. These official documents highlighted the governmental process of returning the rights of agricultural production and operation to the farmers. In 1982, the government acknowledged the legitimacy of the household responsibility system, which empowered farmers to operate their farms autonomously. In 1983, controls over rural industries and enterprises were loosened, allowing the farmers freedom of choice in job selection. In 1984, the channels of commodity distribution were opened, enabling farmers to sell their produce directly to the market. In 1985, the state monopoly for purchasing and supplying produce was removed, further increasing farmers' autonomy. In 1986, investments in agriculture were increased while the industrial-agricultural and urban-rural structures were adjusted to give peasants more guaranteed rights and also ensure equal development.

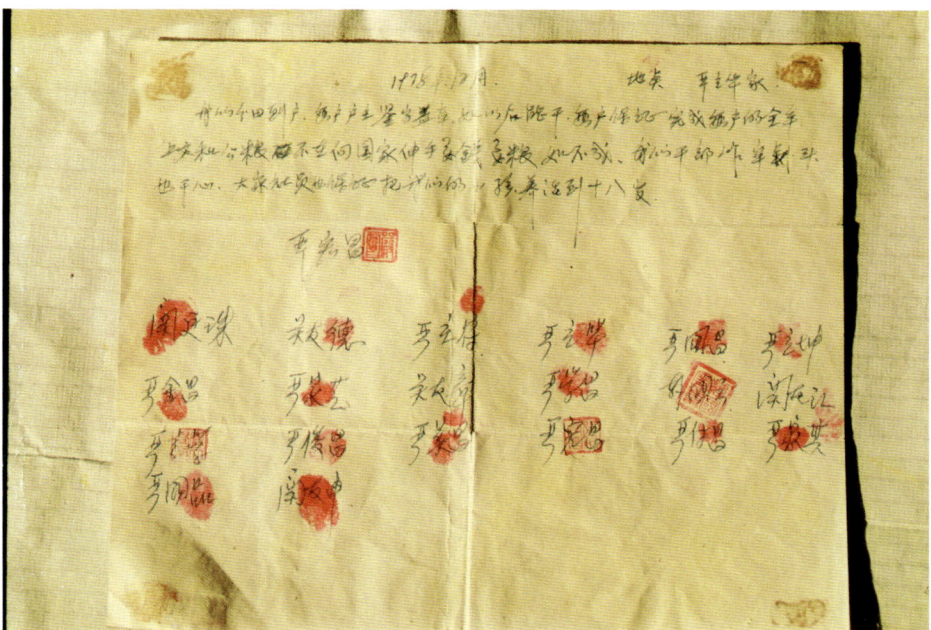

On November 24, 1978, 18 farmers of the Xiaogang Production Team secretly pledged to implement the practice of fixing farm output quotas based on a household basis. In the agreement, they agreed that they would meet the state farm output quotas, give the collective their lots, and keep the rest for themselves.

The rural economic reform improved the performance of China's agricultural economy. Between 1978 and 1985, the total grain output grew from 304.77 million tons to 379.11 million tons, an increase of 24.4%, while cotton output jumped from 2.167 million tons to 4.147 million tons, a rise of 91.4%. The per capita income of peasant households increased from RMB 133.60 to RMB 397.60, a rise of 168.9% in terms of comparable prices.

The significant increase in agricultural output and accompanying rise in peasants' incomes both increased their purchasing power as well as expanded the rural market. As a result, many farmers were able to build new houses and purchase the "four major household appliances": a bicycle, a sewing machine, a radio, and a wrist watch. In addition, the accumulated surplus capital and labor force of the rural townships and villages created a new economic force. Townships and village enterprises were able to greatly increase farmers' income by providing them with new employment opportunities. The success of rural economic reform not only provided an example for reforming urban enterprises, but also created the necessary economic foundations of capital and labor.

As SOEs and peasant households were given more autonomy in production, the reform of the financial management system allowed local governments to utilize their initiative. The central government began to reform the

China's agricultural sector experienced abundant harvests with surplus every year through her reform.

financial management system in 1980 by clarifying the scope of income and expenditure for both central and local finance departments. These steps gave the local government greater autonomy in managing assets and expanded the scope of both their income and expenditure.

Economic reforms and the opening up to the outside world have progressed in tandem. Today, the Chinese government encourages and supports exports as a means of accumulating foreign exchange, actively introduce advanced technologies, utilize foreign capital in multiple forms, and rapidly expand the scale of capital introduction. China has changed her policy of avoiding external and internal debts, and has actively borrowed capital from various lenders throughout the world. The clearest representation of China's opening up to the outside world is the formation of special economic zones (SEZs). In 1980, China designated SEZs in the four coastal cities of Shenzhen, Zhuhai, Shantou, and Xiamen. The distinctiveness of SEZs is reflected in their special economic policies and management systems. SEZs contain both SOEs and collective enterprises, in addition to a large number of Sino-foreign joint ventures and foreign-invested commercial enterprises. SEZs give enterprises greater autonomy coupled with favorable economic policies and preferential benefits. Therefore, they not only serve to attract foreign capital and introduce new technologies, but also function as a testing ground and pathfinder for market reform.

China's process of reform and opening up has progressed in tandem with changes in the international economic environment. During the oil crisis of the 1970s, the developed countries realized that increasing production costs would undermine the competitiveness of their products. Therefore, production costs had to be kept low by better allocating resources globally. One practical alternative was to set up plants in countries and regions where the price of land, raw materials, and labor were relatively cheap. China's opening up of Shenzhen and Zhuhai signaled her intention to attract entrepreneurs from Hong Kong and Macau to set up plants in mainland China. In addition, the nearby cities of Shantou and Xiamen are well-known for their large population of returned overseas Chinese, making them attractive destinations for capital from overseas Chinese investors. Firms from developed economies therefore saw the unique advantages and opportunities in doing business in China.

These four SEZs have made great achievements, especially for Shenzhen. Within a short period of time, Shenzhen transformed herself from a small fishing village into a modern metropolis. The SEZs are the pioneers of urban reform and also offer the local Chinese an opportunity to learn about and understand the world outside China.

Both China's government and her people were inspired by the success of rural reform. At the same time, she created the material basis for further reform. In October 1984, at the Third Plenary Session, the 14th Central Committee of the CPC put forward *The Decision of the Central Committee of the Communist Party of China on Economic System Reform,* which kick-started the full-scale reformation of the economy. The decision gave clear guiding principles for reform, and used the primary stage theory of socialism for its theoretical foundation. Success of economic reforms would no longer be measured by the relations of production, but rather how reform was beneficial to the development of productivity. The role of the market was emphasized, with the central government's economic policies and guidelines pointing out that "the state regulates the market, while the market guides the enterprises." Previously, the elimination of the free market was a target of socialism. Now, the free market was a necessary and beneficial part of the public ownership economy.

Following the guideline of establishing a socialist commodity economy, several key reforms were announced in succession, each reform successively increasing the role of the market in resource allocation. The reforms targeted mandatory planned management within the planning, investment, distribution, financial, and taxation systems. In 1982, the 12th CPC National Congress declared that mandatory planning, guidance planning, and market regulation

Shenzhen SEZ in Guangdong Province is the forerunner of China's opening up and reform.

were all legitimate methods of resource allocation, although the scope of mandatory planning would be gradually narrowed. As the role of government planning shrank and that of the market expanded, a dual pricing system came into effect that included government pricing, government-guided pricing, and free market pricing.

The three major drivers of China's economy are consumption, investments, and exports. During the period of the planned economy, China's economic growth was driven mainly by a high accumulation of capital through investments. The government determined the ratio between capital accumulation and consumption, as well as controlled the deployment of investments based on existing needs. While this method was somewhat rational based on historical circumstances, it was also flawed in many ways. Just as there could be malfunctions in market adjustments, such malfunctions could also happen in government adjustments. Therefore, when the planning system was reformed in 1984, the government took steps to delegate powers to review construction projects, increase investment channels, and diversify sources of capital. In addition, market competition was introduced into the management of investment projects.

Finance is the heart of economic operations; hence financial reform was also inevitable. Since enterprises could not function solely as the government's workshop, banks also could not only be serving as the government's accountant and treasury. As capital is a very important factor of production, financial markets must be set up to enable capital to circulate freely and achieve its maximum marginal return. Banks and firms can also become sources and destinations of supply and demand in financial markets. Banking reforms began in 1979, when the Agricultural Bank of China and the Bank of China were demerged from the People's Bank of China. In 1983, the Industrial and Commercial Bank of China and the China Construction Bank also became independent. Today, the People's Bank of China is no longer involved in commercial financial services; it only regulates monetary policy and maintains the stability of the Renminbi. In the meantime, non-banking financial institutions have also emerged, including the People's Insurance Company of China, the China International Trust and Investment Corporation, and many others.

The distribution system is also markedly different from that of the past. Previously, the government took on the market's role, but now market supply and demand determines distribution, allowing commercial enterprises to perform as rational market actors. The central government has also gradually reduced the number and variety of industrial and agricultural products subjected to price controls. More measures to open up to the outside world were also taken. In April 1984, in recognition of the strong development of the SEZs, the Central Committee of the Communist Party of China (CCCPC) decided to convert 14 port cities of Dalian, Qinhuangdao, Tianjin, Yantai, Qingdao, Lianyungang, Nantong, Shanghai, Ningbo, Wenzhou, Fuzhou, Guangzhou, Zhanjiang, and Beihai into SEZs and therefore quicken the pace of foreign capital utilization and the introduction of advanced technologies. In 1985, the Yangtze River Delta, the Pearl River Delta, and the Min River Delta were designated as national coastal economic open zones. In 1988, the CCCPC designated Jiaodong Peninsula (Shandong) and Liaodong Peninsula (Liaoning) as national coastal economic development zones. In the same year, the Hainan SEZ was established.

These moves caused notable changes to China's economic and social structure. As reforms deepened, various market players came into being while different types of markets developed. The administrative relationship between the central government and SOEs has continuously improved through a process of experimentation. Township and village enterprises have unexpectedly emerged, and with the powerful support of government policies, the private and market economies have grown increasingly larger. Foreign-funded enterprises such as joint ventures, cooperative enterprises, and foreign-invested commercial enterprises have also developed quickly. The benefits of foreign capital and technology introduction are also improving. Through all of these developments, China is becoming more closely connected with the international markets.

The reforms also brought significant changes to China's economic landscape, with GDP rising from RMB 720.8 billion in 1984 to RMB 1.5 trillion in 1988; a 53.4% increase in terms of comparable prices. The structure of the tertiary industry became increasingly efficient as the secondary and tertiary industries grew at a rapid rate. As a result, the Chinese people's living standards also improved consistently. In addition, the total volume of import and export cargo increased from US$53.6 billion in 1984 to US$102.8 billion in 1988. The amount of foreign capital actually utilized rose from US$2.9 billion in 1984 to US$10.2 billion in 1988, with the proportion of foreign direct investments to GDP rising from 0.5% in 1984 to 0.8% in 1988.

As the CPC and the central government carried on the process of reform and opening up, her economic outlook began to mature. In 1985, Deng Xiaoping put forward the concept of the "Two Overall Situations"; in 1987, the 13th CPC National Congress announced the strategic concept of developing the economy in three steps. These concepts provided the Chinese people with tangible goals while enabling China's economy to develop steadfastly.

Alongside the reform process, several problems such as inflation, economic imbalances, corruption, and so on, reared their ugly heads. People became especially concerned about inflation during the "Breakthrough in Price Reform" in 1998. Despite the well-intentioned aim of the "price reform" policy—to solve

FYI
FOR YOUR
INFORMATION

THE CONCEPT OF THE "TWO OVERALL SITUATIONS"

In September 1988, Deng Xiaoping announced that: "The coastal areas must accelerate their opening up to the outside world, so as to enable this vast region with 200 million people to develop in a relatively fast manner, and hence accelerate the development of the inland region—this is the overall situation. The inland regions must understand this overall situation clearly. However, once the inland regions' development reaches a certain level, the coastal areas will still be required to support the inland regions to develop further—this is also an issue concerning the overall situation. When such a time comes, the coastal areas must also conform to this overall situation." These comments were later conceptualized as the "Two Overall Situations." Between the 1980s and the 1990s, the coastal areas were granted many privileges and preferential economic policies while opening up, and at the end of the 1990s, the central government promulgated the policies of "Develop the Western Region" and "Rejuvenate the Industrial Hub of the Northeast"; these policies were all implemented with the "Two Overall Situations" concept in mind.

the problem of distorted prices within market and enterprise reform—it triggered many rounds of panic buying and inflation. The political unrest in 1989 added to the confusion in the economy. Many Chinese people's mindsets were still in the era of the planned economy. It was therefore natural for misunderstood concepts to become prominent during the economic chaos of 1998 and the political unrest in 1989. While on the one hand, those problems gave the Chinese government more experience in governance, on the other hand, they were issues that need to be resolved by the CCCPC.

In early 1992, during his inspection of Wuchang, Shenzhen, Zhuhai, and Shanghai, Deng Xiaoping delivered his famous "Southern Tour" speech. The speech served to further explain the meaning and purpose of reform and opening up. He expounded on the fundamental theoretical principles for establishing a socialist market economy. The speech highlighted the significance of China's reform and opening up as well as her modernization drive. The speech also initiated a new series of "thoughts liberation," breaking down people's tendency to think in polarized terms of "socialism" versus "capitalism." It was in this environment that in 1992, the 14th CPC National Congress established the goal of creating a socialist market economy system. In November 1993, the Third Plenary Session of the 14th CCCPC passed the *Decision on Several Issues Regarding the Establishment of a Socialist Market Economy System*. From 1992, a series of reforms was initiated to target the finance and taxation, banking, foreign exchange, foreign trade, planning, and investment sectors. At the same time, further efforts were made to better define the relationship between the government, the market, and enterprises, while improving the system of macroeconomic regulation.

The movement toward economic globalization and regionalization has become increasingly apparent since the 1990s. China must further integrate herself into the global community if she hopes to achieve her development goals. After years of development, China had successfully established a buyer's market in 1997, marking the end of shortages in the economy and making inadequate supply a thing of the past. The focus of economic development shifted from the issue of inadequate supply to the matter of inadequate demand. To this end, the central government changed the regulatory direction of macroeconomic policy, unveiling a series of policies and measures that sought to increase domestic demand and consumption.

In 1997, the 15th CPC National Congress made the following proposals regarding the direction of economic development and structural evolution:

- adjust and improve the ownership structure;
- promote the reform of state-owned enterprises;
- improve the distribution structure and allocation method;
- allow full utilization of market mechanisms;
- strengthen the system of macroeconomic regulation;
- reinforce agriculture as a fundamental base;
- adjust and optimize the economic structure;
- implement the strategies of "Invigorating China through Science and Education"; and "Sustainable Development"; and
- improve the process of opening up to the outside world.

The Chinese government implemented her twin economic policies of "expanding domestic demand" and "preventing financial risks," which included active financial policies and firm currency policies as well as other relevant measures such as health care, housing, and education reform. In the later half of 1998, the welfare-based system of public housing allocation ended. Hence, the percentage of residents purchasing commercial housing increased. The social security system was also established and improved. In 1999, in order to mitigate financial risks, the central government established China Cinda Asset Management Corporation, China Orient Asset Management Corporation, China Huarong Asset Management Corporation, and China Great Wall Asset Management Corporation, which purchased and managed the non-performing assets of the four major state-owned commercial banks. Meanwhile, financial supervision was strengthened.

In 1997, the Asian financial crisis temporarily set back the progress of China's economic development, but the government promptly adopted effective measures to prevent the stagnation of the economy. Large and middle-sized SOEs emerged from the crisis and accomplished the goal of "shaking off poverty in three years." Meanwhile, private firms also achieved significant growth. The economic structure continued to progress and the people's standard of living improved. The target of quadrupling China's per capita income was achieved ahead of schedule, and China became a relatively prosperous society.

After successfully developing a buyer's market in 1997 and quadrupling the national economy, China began to focus on narrowing the gap between coastal and inland regions, particularly the Western Region, which became a means for increasing domestic demand. In 1999, the central government promulgated the "Develop the Western Region" strategy, and formulated corresponding economic policies and measures. The central provinces immediately adopted the motto of "Emergence of Central China."

Upon entering the twenty-first century, the reform of China's socialist market system made further progress and breakthroughs. Capital, technology, and labor markets were further standardized and developed. In 2002, China's

Since the 1990s, China witnessed the growth of the stock markets, with an ever-growing number of stock investors.

national bonds market, securities market, and funds market all made considerable progress. The real estate market began to play a progressively important role in fuelling investment, and its contribution toward GDP became larger and larger. Meanwhile, China integrated further into the global economic system, most markedly with her accession into the WTO in 2001 to become its 143rd member.

In 2001, China's successful bid for the hosting of the 2008 Olympic Games further enhanced domestic and international confidence in China's long term stable growth, jumpstarting an increase in both investment and consumption the following year. The construction of Beijing's Olympic stadiums and other infrastructure projects in 2002 increased investments and further fuelled China's GDP growth.

In 2002, China also began to reap benefits from her accession to the WTO, with overseas investors enthusiastically rushing into China. For the first time, China was ranked number one in the world in terms of attracting foreign direct investments. Meanwhile, exports continued to enjoy significant growth, which was the main driving force behind China's GDP growth. The benefits of WTO membership not only spurred economic growth that year, but also further promoted the structural reform of the economy. China also continued her in-depth economic reform in line with established international standards, with the pace of reform and adjustment of the economic structure advancing side by side.

In 2002, the CPC convened the 16th CPC National Congress, where it announced the goal of building a relatively prosperous society during the first 20 years of the twenty-first century. The CPC announced its intention to further develop the economy, improve democracy, promote science and education, enrich cultural elements, and bring about a more harmonious society while raising the people's living standards. The CPC's fundamental strategy in building a relatively prosperous society was to adhere to the central mission of economic development, while continually liberating and increasing productivity. To fulfill the above-mentioned development targets while taking into account resource, environmental, and population restraints, it was clearly not feasible to continue adhering to the original developmental concepts and approaches.

Coordinated Development Based on the Scientific Outlook on Development (2003–2010)

As China's economy improves and the processes of industrialization and urbanization accelerate, the energy and environmental challenges facing China's economic development have also grown. Consequently, the need to alter China's approach to economic development has become increasingly prominent. China's sustainable economic development and continued leadership role in global development depends on whether her approach to economic growth can transition from being externally-oriented to internally-oriented.

China is a large developing country with imbalanced conditions of economic development. She faces low levels of per capita resources, complex and diverse geographic conditions, and an imbalanced distribution of resources and population. Years of reform and opening up have enabled China's economy to achieve overall rapid development. However, the developmental differences between urban and rural areas, and coastal and inland regions continue to widen, in addition to the income gap between the rich and the poor.

Furthermore, the Chinese government faces complex problems involving the implementation of in-depth reform, delineating the relationship between the state and the market, and transforming and standardizing the central government's functions.

In 2003, China faced a sudden and shocking outbreak of a Severe Acute Respiratory Syndrome (SARS) epidemic, which crippled some sectors and retarded economic growth. However, this incident did not have any effect on China's modernization drive. Within a year, China overcame the impact of SARS, droughts, floods, and the pressure of the Renminbi appreciation to achieve sustained and rapid development. At the same time, China made positive progress in adjusting the structure of the economy and raising the standard of living. Meanwhile, the state utilized its successful handling of SARS to reform government organizations.

The year 2003 saw China begin her trial tax reforms in rural areas. This effort marked the most significant change in the relationship between the government and the farmers since the implementation of the household contract responsibility system in 1978. The government also focused its attention on developing both West and Northeast China with the twin strategies of "Develop the Western Region" and "Rejuvenate the Industrial Hub of the Northeast," thereby accelerating the coordinated development of different regional economies.

Throughout 2003, China's industrialization entered a new phase, propelled by the growth of the manufacturing industry, upgrading of the industrial structure, industrialization of advanced technologies, and opening up to the outside world. All these factors promoted the strong growth of China's economy, minimizing the effects of any obstruction to China's pace of modernization. Events in the same year demonstrated that in the face of tremendous challenges involving the population, resources, the environment and economic coordination, China needed to follow a new path of industrialization. Furthermore, she had to focus on resolving issues related to finance, SOEs, agriculture, the countryside, and the farmers among other things.

In 2003, confronted with these issues, tasks, and challenges, the Third Plenary Session of the 16th CCCPC announced several new concepts to guide its economic development, namely the "people-oriented" Scientific Outlook on Development, and proposed to coordinate China's overall social and economic development with the "Five Comprehensive Plans." They are the comprehensive plans of:

- urban and rural development;
- regional development;
- economic and social development;
- harmonious development between humans and the environment; and
- domestic development and opening up to the outside world.

Development with a "people-oriented" core approach was the primary objective of the Scientific Outlook on Development. With fundamental standards of overall coordination and sustainability, the concept's basic methodology was to create comprehensive plans that took all factors into consideration. These five aspects were interlinked and organically unified; the principle was to realize a better and faster economic and social development.

In 2004, the Fourth Plenary Session of the 16th CCCPC again put forward the vision of building a harmonious society. A more harmonious society was an important and fundamental part of building a relatively prosperous society. The emphasis at this meeting was on the significance of a harmonious society in China's economic development. A harmonious society is a society characterized by democracy and the rule of law, fairness and justice, credibility and fraternity, abundant vitality, peace and order, and harmonious co-existence between humans and nature. To build such a society, it was essential to fully implement the Scientific Outlook on Development and utilize its spirit in all aspects of economic and social development.

Besides that, 2004 was the Year of the Scientific Outlook on Development in China. People increasingly adopted this new mode of thinking. The concepts of being "people-oriented, comprehensive, coordinated, and sustainable" have all grown deep inside people's minds. The idea had changed the previous method of increasing the overall GDP growth by promoting only particular sectors. This became the ultimate criterion for measuring the standard and quality of development.

At the same time, 2004 was also the Year of the Farmers. After 18 years, the central government once again focused on the "agriculture, the countryside and farmers" issue in the spirit of the No.1 Document. Guided by the concept of the "city supporting the countryside with the industry supporting agriculture" and with the aid of the "Two Exemptions, Three Subsidies"[1] policy, 900 million farmers began to realize the tangible benefits from the reform. The amount of land under grain cultivation ended the worrying trend of continual decline for many years. An increase in grain production also recorded its highest rise in 10 years, and the income of grain producing farmers showed significant improvements.

Furthermore, 2004 was a landmark year for China in terms of strengthening and improving her macroeconomic regulation. It was also an exemplary year where economic development and social campaigns achieved new heights. The central government adopted a series of measures to strengthen and improve macroeconomic regulation, enabling China's economy to maintain a healthy pace of steady and relatively fast growth, thus extending the ascendant stage of the economic cycle.

In 2005, the CCCPC once again selected the issue of "agriculture, the countryside, and farmers" as the subject of its No.1 Document. Meanwhile, with the successful launch of the *Shenzhou VI* manned spaceship, China further highlighted the importance of innovation. The reform plans for Renminbi foreign exchange, equity division, and public listing of commercial banks among others were initiated and introduced. China's economy maintained stable growth, with the price level index growing steadily, and financial aid to agriculture improving. Throughout the year, the government's macroeconomic regulation stressed specific guarantee and specific control, while fixed asset investment (FAI) maintained a high growth rate and increased by 20%. Investments and consumption, especially in real estate and automobile industries gradually rose; domestic demand accelerated growth as pro-consumption policies came into effect.

In 2006, at the Fifth Plenary Session of the 16th CCCPC, it was declared that building a new socialist countryside was a key historic task in the course of China's modernization drive. Based on the requirements of "production development, prosperous life, civilized living in the counties, neat and tidy village surroundings, and democratic management," it was essential to adhere to the practice of improving living conditions, respecting farmers' wishes, and steadfastly promoting the building of a new countryside.

A critical part of China's development plans for urban and rural areas was the building of a new socialist countryside. The plan takes into account China's historical conditions and is part of the implementation procedure of the guidelines for "industry nurturing agriculture and cities supporting the countryside."

---

[1]Exemption of agricultural tax, cancellation of agricultural special duty excluding tobacco, direct subsidy to grain farmers, subsidy toward high-yield seeds, and subsidy toward purchase of agricultural machinery, and tools for farmers of some areas.

This picture shows a village in Ganxian County, Jiangxi Province, taken in February 2006.

The agricultural tax, which had existed in China for more than 2,000 years, was completely abolished at the beginning of 2006, thereby relieving farmers of a tax burden of RMB 126.5 billion. Upon the abolishment of the agricultural tax, China's agricultural sector and labor relations entered a new age. Technological innovation again took center stage in 2006 at the National Science and Technology Conference, when China introduced the strategic target of creating an innovation-oriented nation.

In 2006, China's 11th Five-Year Plan for economic and social development was approved. Compared with the 10th Five-Year Plan and other previous five-year plans, both the form and concepts of economic reform in the 11th Five-Year Plan have undergone revolutionary changes. The "Getting Rich First Theory" (i.e., allowing certain people in certain regions with the right conditions to become prosperous first), which had played a major role in the developmental concept of China's reform and opening up for over 20 years, was transformed into the "Getting Rich Together Theory" (i.e., the people and regions that became rich first should help other people or other regions to progressively realize common prosperity). This theory aimed to narrow the gap between the rich and the poor and reverse the trend of polarization of the society. The theory has become the new subject of economic development. Furthermore, the change from a planned economy to planning the economy

In 2006, the 2000-year-old agriculture tax was finally abolished. Chinese farmers benefited enormously from this new policy.

highlights the fundamental change in the central government's way of managing the economy. This reflects the supreme realm of the Scientific Outlook on Development.

China transited from a philosophy of "Speed and Quality" in 2005 to one of "Quality and Speed" in 2006. In 2007, the Central Economic Working Conference decreed that in the following year, economic results must place priority on quality. The importance of "quality" is continuously growing in China's economic development policies and measures, which reflects the determination of the central government to transform the structure of economic growth, and achieve comprehensive, coordinated, and sustainable development of the economy.

China aims to become a world leader in environmental protection by conserving energy and reducing pollution. Shops and markets across China have now stopped giving out free plastic shopping bags and consumers are now encouraged to bring their own recyclable bags.

China has maintained a strong growth rate and kept pace with the global economy since the beginning of the twenty-first century, while keeping inflation at a low rate. Nevertheless, in 2007, the inflationary pressures increased. "Preventing the structural rise of prices from evolving into inflation" became the central task of the Chinese government's macroeconomic regulation. In order to reduce currency liquidity, the government also tried to restrain a rapid rise in prices and stock market bubbles by raising the interest rate and letting the Renminbi appreciate.

2007 was the turning point for China's energy conservation and emissions reductions. In the first three quarters, energy consumption per nationwide unit of GDP dropped by 3%, while the discharge of sulfur dioxide and COD both fell for the first time in history. This offered hope to the Chinese people in their efforts to reach the 11th Five-Year Plan overall target, which was to achieve a 20% reduction in energy consumption per unit of GDP and a 10% reduction in main emissions between 2006 and 2010.

Facing new trends and an evolving situation, the 17th CPC National Congress further outlined the targets and strategies for China's economic development. The congress introduced new requirements for attaining the goal of building a relatively prosperous society:

- strengthen coordination in development;
- strive to achieve healthy and rapid development;
- make significant progress in transforming and structurally optimizing the development approach;
- improve benefits;
- reduce energy consumption;
- protect the environment; and
- achieve the target of quadrupling per capita GDP by 2020 compared to 2000.

To reach this grand target, it was important to improve the efficiency of the modern market system; optimize the pattern of national land development; deepen finance, taxation, and banking system reform; and speed up the transformation of the economic development pattern.

China's countryside and farmers are major issues of concern, and must be addressed with regard to China's goal of building a prosperous society. The report of the 17th CPC National Congress specifically stressed the importance of making a comprehensive plan for urban and rural development, and promoting the construction of a new socialist countryside. It made these goals a top priority in the CPC's work, reflecting the CCCPC's goal of people-oriented and effective governance.

In 2008, the Chinese people experienced an unusual year due to the effects of natural disasters and the global financial crisis. Sudden changes in the international prices of bulk commodities as well as the progressive deterioration of the global financial system occurred. Furthermore, "rollercoaster" fluctuations in the global economy had a significant effect on China's economy. Meanwhile, natural disasters such as the blizzard at the beginning of the year and the earthquake in Sichuan Province also exerted unexpected pressure on the world's biggest emerging market, which had maintained double-digit growth rates for five consecutive years.

In order to deal with new economic developments, China introduced appropriate macroeconomic regulatory policies so as to guarantee steady and fast economic growth (her growth rate was approaching 8.7%). At the beginning of 2008, the officials implemented the "Double Protection" policy, which aimed to prevent overheating of the economy and rapid inflation. In the middle of the same year, they implemented the "Maintain and Control" policy, which aimed to strike a balance between growth and inflation. In September 2008, the central government implemented the "Guaranteed Growth" policy and two months later, the "Guaranteed Growth and Expand Domestic Demand" policy. The final policy of 2008 was the "Guarantee Growth, Expand Domestic Demand, and Restructuring" at the Central Economic Working Conference. The effective and timely changes in policies highlighted the important role of the government in maintaining the stability of China's economy during those tumultuous times.

If 2008 was a very difficult year for China's economy, her economy faced even more grim challenges in 2009. In 2008, when the blizzard resulted in a shortage of coal and power, some Chinese enterprises sought to reduce costs by stockpiling large quantities of inventory in anticipation of a price rise in the global market. Such stockpiling of inventory will reduce demand. Meanwhile, the sharp decline in exports—one of the three key driving forces fueling GDP growth in China for many years—will also present serious economic challenges. In order to prevent significant economic fluctuations, China needed to further expand both investment and domestic consumption.

In response to the need to stimulate investment and domestic consumption, the Chinese government introduced a stimulus plan. It mainly consisted of four items:

(1) large-scale government investments (total amount of RMB 4 trillion over two years, of which central government investment accounts for RMB 1.18 trillion;
(2) large-scale industry adjustment and revitalization;
(3) widespread support for advanced technologies; and
(4) significant improvement of the social security system.

The Chinese government was confident of reaching 8% GDP growth in 2009. There were several contributing factors. Firstly, China's industrialization, marketization, and urbanization were all in stages of accelerated development, while the structure of domestic consumption was upgrading and expanding. There are 700 million farmers among China's 1.3 billion people. In terms of either population or regional criteria, the Chinese market is naturally one of the most important markets in the world. Secondly, China boasts competitive advantages in abundant labor resources and skills. Thirdly, after over 30 years of reform and opening up, especially the financial system reform over the past 10 years, China's financial system is fundamentally healthy and stable, and serves as a powerful support pillar for the nation's economic development.

FYI
FOR YOUR INFORMATION

CHINA'S FOUR TRILLION RENMINBI INVESTMENT

In November 2008, in order to cope with the increasingly serious global financial crisis and mitigate its adverse impact on China, the government decided to implement a proactive financial policy and a moderately loose monetary policy. The central government unveiled 10 measures that aimed at expanding domestic demand, including accelerating projects to improve people's living standards, infrastructure, ecological and environmental development, post-disaster reconstruction, among other things. The implementation of these 10 measures required an investment of approximately RMB 4 trillion by end-2010.

The RMB 4 trillion investments are equivalent to 13.3% of China's economy and 23% of 2008's investment sums. Out of this investment, new investments by the central government will total RMB 1.18 trillion, accounting for 29.5% of the total investment sum, the bulk of which comes from the central government's investment budget, expenditure funds, and other public investments from the central budget, in addition to the post-disaster recovery and reconstruction fund. Investment from other sources will total RMB 2.82 trillion, accounting for 70.5% of total invested sum, the bulk of which comes from local budgets, local government bonds issued by the central finance department, policy-driven loans, enterprise bonds and medium-term notes, bank loans, private investment, and so on.

The RMB 4 trillion investment can be broken down into these main areas:

1. Projects to improve people's living standards, which mainly include welfare housing projects such as low-rent housing, reforestation and reclamation in some areas, and rejuvenation of coal mining areas. The total invested sum is about RMB 400 billion.

2. Projects to improve the people's living standards in rural areas, including infrastructure for water, electricity, roads, gas, and housing. The focus is on providing safe potable water, renovating the existing power grid, building roads, building more marsh gas facilities, renovating dilapidated buildings, and relocating nomadic herders. The total invested sum is about RMB 370 billion.

3. Construction projects of infrastructure facilities, railways, highways, airports, hydraulic engineering projects, among others. The total investment sum is about RMB 1.5 trillion.

4. Social projects that focus on improving education, health care, culture, family planning, and so on. The total investment sum is about RMB 150 billion.

5. Projects relating to energy conservation and emissions reduction, ecological engineering, among others. The total invested sum is about RMB 210 billion.

6. Structural and technical renovations. The total investment sum is about RMB 370 billion.

7. Post-disaster restoration and reconstruction, particularly in the key disaster areas of the Sichuan Earthquake. The total investment sum is about RMB 1 trillion.

In the first quarter of 2009, the investment-expanding measures listed above began to show solid economic results; central government investment accelerated the total growth in fixed asset investments, resulting in a strong pickup in key investment areas and sectors. At the same time, economic operations improved, while industrial production and the prices of some investment commodities gradually stabilized.

Policies implemented and measures taken by the Chinese government have been accurate and effective. According to the latest data released on October 22, 2009, by the National Statistics Bureau, China witnessed a GDP increase of 7.7% in the first three quarters of 2009, in which the third quarter saw an 8.9% increase year-on-year. Meanwhile, the spokesman of the bureau also commented that China's economic stimulus package has shown obvious effects. The economy stabilized and staged a significant recovery, making the target of 8% growth for 2009 a certainty.

On July 22, 2009, in view of the fact that some leading indexes of the Chinese economy have made a turn for the better. The International Monetary Fund (IMF) indicated that, according to recent data, China's economy had started to recover ahead of other countries. The IMF also praised the Chinese government's proactive financial and monetary policies that helped to mitigate the economic downturn. These policies will both facilitate economic recovery in 2009 and 2010 and make a contribution to global economic stability. In its *China Quarterly Update* released on November 4, 2009, the World Bank subsequently changed its forecast from the original 7.2% to 8.4%, and indicated that

Though affected by the world financial crisis, China witnessed a GDP increase of 7.7% in the first three quarters of 2009, becoming a world leader in magnitude, thanks to the effective and targeted economic measures.

this was a result of the unexpected effect caused by China's economic stimulus packages. On December 2, 2009, the UN released ahead of schedule the main contents of its report *World Economic Situation and Prospects in 2010*. The report stated that the global economy would slowly recover with 2.4% slow growth in 2010, if the current economic stimulus package could be sustained. The developing economies would become the major economic powerhouses for the global economy in 2010, in which the developing economies in Asia will see the most rapid increases. The economies of China and India were expected to increase 8.8% and 5.6%, respectively. This shows that China had once again taken the lead of the world's economic recovery.

Despite these successes, the Chinese government remained cautious. On July 23, 2009, the Politburo of the CCCPC convened a meeting and concluded that there were still unstable factors in the current economy. Therefore, they decided to continue to adopt policies that promote steady and relatively fast economic development, this being the primary task of China's economic plan in the later half of 2009.

The Central Economic Working Conference was held in Beijing during December 5–7, 2009. The successes and failures of China's economy in 2009 were summarized, and the economic work plan for 2010 was finalized. It was stated at the conference that the central government would be focused on promoting the transition of mode of development, expanding domestic demand, particularly increasing residents' consumptions in an effort to boost urbanization, optimize industrial structure, and strive for substantial achievements in economic structural re-adjustments. Meanwhile, China will maintain the continuity and stability of her macroeconomic policies in 2010, continue with the implementation of a proactive fiscal policy and a moderately easy monetary policy. The outlook for China remains optimistic such that the conference can be used to promote the nation's economic stability and recovery, and speed up the re-adjustment of her economic structure.

Chapter 3

China's Basic Economic System and Policies

After more than 30 years of reform and opening up, China's economic system has undergone significant transformations that are vastly different from the obsolete system used before 1978. Between 1949 and 1978, the transitional goal of China's economic system was to build up and improve the socialist planned economy. Today, the transitional goal of China's economic system is to build a socialist market economy. Throughout the process of systemic transition, China's economic system has developed a unique set of essential characteristics through her inheritance of an ancient culture, the utilization of practical experience, and the borrowing of advanced technology and expertise from overseas.

A Socialist Market Economy with Chinese Characteristics

The goal of China's economic development is to set up a socialist market economy, which is also the most basic path toward achieving China's goals of

The market economy introduced more choices of daily necessities to the Chinese people.

industrialization, urbanization, and modernization. This brings into play the special characteristics of China's current socialist economy. It is completely different from the socialist economic system before 1978, which was characterized by singular public ownership and a planned economy.

After the founding of the People's Republic of China in 1949, and in consideration of the international and domestic environment, the government progressively established a highly centralized planned economy. As the size and scale of such a planned economic system changes, so does its efficiency. With conditions such as low information costs, a singular demand and commodity supply structure, there was a certain amount of rationality in planning the allocation of resources. However, as the economic system expanded and became increasingly complex along with the structure of consumption and demand and the diversification of products, the drawbacks of the planned economy soon became obvious.

The drawbacks of China's planned economic system were primarily manifested in the following elements:

(1) The forms of ownership became increasingly singular, with public ownership dominating the economic system to the exclusion of all other forms of ownership. In the public ownership economy, state-owned enterprises occupied a dominant position.

(2) For the operation and management of the state economy, regardless of whether it was a state-owned enterprise or collective enterprise, the rights of operation and decision-making were under the charge of several levels of government, leading enterprises to become an extension of government bureaucracies and therefore lose their independence and function, merely acting as a workshop within the gigantic enterprise of government. The official methods of managing the economy relied heavily on administrative approaches, through administrative decrees and the distribution of real goods, and allocation of resources.

(3) The market was weak in allocating resources, and in some cases, it completely failed in this regard.

(4) Income was distributed through a highly centralized and planned management system, which not only included SOEs "eating from the same big pot" as the state, but also staff members "eating from the same big pot" (*Da Guo Fan*) of the enterprise. Within the collective economy, an egalitarian distribution method was implemented in which members received the same compensation regardless of the quantity and quality of their work. As a result, both enterprises and individuals lacked initiative in production.

China's 30 years of experience before the reform and opening up has proven that a singular public ownership system and a planned economy were increasingly contradicting the needs and sometimes obstructed economic development. Consequently, the CPC and the Chinese government started to experiment and explore models for a systemic reform of the economic system. As there was no readily available model to adopt or prior experience to apply, the classic Chinese method of "crossing the river by feeling the stones" was used to work through the complicated process of economic reform. This process

"EATING FROM THE SAME BIG POT" (DA GUO FAN)

Da Guo Fan or literally "eating from the same big pot" refers to the fact that all job functions and units in the SOEs under a planned economy system did not operate according to market economic principles. Incentives were not linked to profits regardless of whether a firm makes profits or losses, everyone relied on the state, as if they eating from the state's "big pot."

of exploration was also accompanied by a gradual shift in opinions regarding the relationship between planning and the market.

During the outset of China's reform, spanning the period from 1978 to 1984, China allowed the private economy a certain amount of control in the areas of production and distribution while adhering to a public ownership model. These allowances were made based on the realistic and practical thinking of Deng Xiaoping's concepts of "it doesn't matter what color a cat is, as long as it hunts mice" and "allow some people to get rich first."

The economy as managed by the government was not a completely planned economy as it was in the past, but instead focused on bringing into play the functions of market adjustment, particularly with regard to implementing a planned commodity economy. However, at that time, people's general mindset was not as open, and they were not sufficiently daring to break out of the general framework of a planned economy. The market adjustment only provided auxiliary functions, as described at that time to be "based on planned management, supplemented by market adjustment."

The introduction of market mechanisms inevitably caused contradictions and confrontations when brought into contact with a planned economic system. Therefore, in 1984, the CCCPC introduced a planned commodity economy. This move re-introduced the concept that the nature of the socialist economy was nonetheless a commodity economy. In 1987, the 13th CPC National Congress further recognized the importance of the socialist economy and declared that the target of reform was to center on "the state regulating the market, and the market guiding the firms"; the market then came to be recognized as having a critical role to play in the economic adjustment.

The economy overheated in 1988 and the subsequent recovery and rejuvenation led to people's demands for a stronger macroeconomic regulation and management by the government. The importance of planned management once again became prominent, but the process of marketization reform did not undergo any formal changes. In fact, around this time, people's demand for planned management evolved into a demand for macroeconomic regulation by the state.

After experimentation and experience in the practice and theory of both the positive and negative aspects of reform, China targeted to implement a socialist market economy in 1992. Establishing a socialist market economy required three supporting pillars, namely:

(1) formation of a market body in which multiple economic components can co-exist and a modern enterprise system with a joint-stock system as its core;

(2) development of a microeconomic operating mechanism in which the market determines price and plays a fundamental role in the allocation of resources; and

(3) establishment of a macroeconomic regulatory system in which finance and banking act as two key levers.

Under such an economic system, the function of the market in resource allocation is not only reinforced, but also plays a key role. Compared with the planned economy system, the above three changes constitute a fundamental systemic reform.

The socialist market economy system is associated with China's essential national characteristics, unique historical qualities, and contemporary developmental stage. Furthermore, it meets the Chinese people's demand for a socialist system. Consequently, apart from the basic elements of a market economy, there are also several other features that differ from other nations' market economies.

Firstly, public ownership still enjoys a dominant position over private ownership. China's socialist market economy operates under the dominance of public ownership and joint development of multiple economic elements including the private economy. This is different from any market

On March 5, 2009, the Second Session of the 11th National People's Congress was held in the Great Hall. The purpose was to discuss the government work report made by the Premier of the State Council and to review the State Council's report on the implementation of the National Economic and Social Development Plan of 2008. In addition, the congress reviewed the draft of the National Economic and Social Development Plan of 2009 and reported on the execution of the budgets of the central and local governments of 2008, as well as the drafted budget of the central and local governments of 2009.

economy based on private ownership of the means of production. In fact, as marketization reform progressed, the image of public ownership has gradually changed. For instance, in 1997, the 15th CPC National Congress enlarged the role of public ownership in joint-stock enterprises that were dominated by state-owned shares. Nevertheless, it also differs from the conditions of Western capitalist countries. It was an unprecedented and innovative process to implement a market economy while retaining the dominant influence of public ownership.

Secondly, the CPC's political practice of consulting with other parties forms the political basis for the operation of the socialist market economy. In a large nation like China, regardless of the level of industrialization and modernization, the state of national reunification and territorial integrity, the unity of the population, the harmony of the society, and the development of democracy, everything requires the leadership of a powerful political party. Without a political party with a strong capability for governance and ability to achieve modernization in the interest of the Chinese people, a country will hardly be able to achieve her goals of industrialization and modernization, nor can she effectively guarantee unification of the nation. The experience since the reform and opening up has proven that the CPC not only has the ability to enable the Chinese people to advance, but also make them wealthy. Adopting a socialist market economy system is the only way for the Chinese people to realize great rejuvenation. As it is an arduous undertaking that requires innovation and enterprise, there must be strong macroeconomic regulation by the government in order to create a stable, safe, orderly, and impartial social and economic environment for the market economy.

Thirdly, the ultimate goal of China's socialist market economy is to achieve equity and justice in the society as well as prosperity for everybody. Achieving equity and justice have long been the goals for humankind in their pursuit of a better society. Confucius once said that "the lord of a state or head of a family is concerned about unequal distribution instead of scarcity. He should be concerned with discontentment instead of poverty. When there is equal distribution, poverty will cease, and when there is harmony, scarcity will disappear. Finally, when there is contentment, there will be no revolt." Equity and justice in society is a key task and the essential requirement of socialism with unique Chinese characteristics, along with achieving common prosperity for all people. Although the implementation of a market economy creates relative gaps in income, allowing some people to get rich first also encourages them to help others to get rich later, thus fulfilling the ultimate goal of common prosperity.

Collaboration between the Government and the Market

The relationship between the government and the market plays an important role in every country. This relationship also features strongly in economic theories.

In China, the government played a larger role in the early years of the planned economy era. During that period, national security issues were prominent and the economy therefore bore the characteristics of a war economy. Moreover, the size of the nation's economy was small, information costs were relatively low, and the society's supply and demand structures were also relatively simple. In addition, China faced an external environment full of uncertainties, and had to focus on developing heavy industries and national defense to gain a foothold on the world stage. For this reason, she needed a powerful organization to allocate resources. Indeed, the government is the most powerful organization.

It has been proven that the government allocation of resources in the early days of China's economic construction accomplished her historic mission. China has established an independent industrial system that stands tall among other nations. At a time of continuous international obstruction, China accumulated the capital needed for her industrialization through the development of agriculture as well as foreign exchange earned through export.

As the national economy expanded and the consumption and supply structures grew increasingly complex, the government began to meet rising costs in her information collection. However, the shortcomings of government-led resource allocation became increasingly evident. Therefore, since 1978, when China started her reform and opening up, the government has gradually increased the market's autonomy in microeconomic operations and allowing market mechanisms to play an increasingly fundamental role in resource allocation in her economic development.

Such an institutional change has allowed China to make remarkable achievements in economic development. Economic indicators of China such as agriculture, tertiary industries and foreign trade, total GDP and GDP per capita have shown substantial jumps compared to 30 years ago. In 2008, China became the world's third-largest economy after the United States and Japan. The Chinese people's living standards have been improving steadily and the entire society has become more stable and harmonious.

The history of economic development in the West has proved that the government and the market can play different roles under different historical circumstances. China's industrial structure and economic system are both in transition, so good coordination between the roles of the government and the market is essential. China's institutional changes are oriented toward a socialist market economy system and the role of the market as the basic system for allocating resources goes without question. Judging by the standards of a market economy, China is already a market economy with production factor markets and product markets in which prices for most commodities are determined by the relation between supply and demand in such markets. Only prices of a few essential commodities involving national security or people's livelihood are still government-controlled. However, China still faces the task of realizing further marketization. For example, further improvements are required to bring the credit system, legal system as well as economic order in line with the market economy.

The government has indeed played a considerable role in the transition process. Firstly, China's market-oriented reform is not only a process of transition from the previous planned economy to the current market economy, but also a process of industrialization and urbanization. Economic and social conflicts are a complicated part of this process, which entails the cultivation of market players, changes in people's behavior and thoughts, as well as the establishment of a sound market order. All these require the government to play a specific leading and dominant role.

Secondly, China not only has a vast territory and geographical conditions that vary greatly, but also many regional differences in aspects such as ethnicity, culture, lifestyle, and stage of economic development, which date back to over thousands of years ago. China is such a large country that she needs a unified and strong government at the helm of her economy. The reunification of Hong Kong and Macau with China could not have gone smoothly and also the "one country, two administrative systems" policy would not have been implemented successfully without the power of a strong central government. Similarly, "Develop the Western Region," "Rejuvenate the Industrial Hub of the Northeast," "Emergence of Central China" and other regional economic development strategies are also inseparable from the coordination between the central government and local governments.

China's reform does not only involve her economic system, but also her political system. As Deng Xiaoping once said, without the backing of the political system, the reform of the economic system cannot succeed.

As China is a large country of 1.3 billion people, the reform of the political system must be advanced under strong leadership and carried out one step at a time. The absence of a strong leader and certain steps will inevitably lead to chaotic "pseudo-democracy." Such "democracy" would not guarantee the true interests of the Chinese people and would also go against the sustainable development of China's economy.

Stressing the role of the government does not deny or undermine the market. On the contrary, the fundamental role of the market has constantly improved and strengthened along with market-oriented reforms. In the process of transition and maintaining stable economic growth, the Chinese government not only monitors and regulates the market and maintains market order, but also competes in certain market economic activities, such as planning of industrial investment and infrastructure construction through government investment. Thus, this arrangement will stimulate economic growth and economic activities related to national security and natural monopoly. As the economy continues to grow larger and her market system improves continuously, the status of the government as a competitor will be weakened gradually. As government finance at all levels has been transformed from the "construction-oriented finance" in the past to "service-oriented finance," their role has also been changed from a competitor to a watchdog. China is, without doubt, a country dominated by public enterprises, so the government will still participate in the management of SOEs in the role of a client. However, as markets for factors of production such as labor, real estate, financial and technology markets are standardized continuously and a unified and orderly national market system is being built, the role of the market will gradually increase.

The Chinese government's macroeconomic control has delivered results through the country's central bank, the People's Bank of China. The central bank also decides on financial and monetary policies.

China's market-oriented reform is still ongoing and China is still in the midst of transition. The government and the market need to coordinate with each other and work together. China's market economy is different from that of the developed countries in the West, and the relationship between the Chinese government and the market is also different from that of the Western countries. The government has to fully assume the role of a stabilizing force in China's economic development, as well as encourage the market to take on the fundamental role of resource allocation. The government plays her part in the market; while the market is subjected to government regulations. The two players complement each other perfectly.

Collaboration between the Central Government and Local Governments

China is a multi-ethnic country with a vast territory. The differences in various regions are not only found in geographical conditions, but also in many aspects such as industrial structure, level of economic development, ethnicity, language, cultural heritage, and lifestyle. In some regions, the level of economic development has been relatively high, while in other areas, it is relatively low. The extremely uneven economic development has been one of the basic characteristics of China's economy since the founding of modern China. Currently, China has 34 provincial-level administrative regions, of which medium-sized provinces have populations and land areas rivaling those of large European countries.

In a vast and richly diverse country such as China, the bureaucratic relationship between the central and local governments has always been an important issue for the Chinese government. The divestment of power and authority to local governments is also an issue faced by the central government. It is vital to concentrate on the strength of the central government in order to scale greater heights. It is also important to increase the nimbleness of local governments by delegating certain administrative authority to them. Naturally, as the local governments' power increases, local protectionism and excessive and unhealthy competition among regions may appear, and gaps in economic development between regions may widen, resulting in instability and disharmony throughout China's society.

In the era of planned economy before reform and opening up, China was in a constant and repetitive cycle of "delegation" and "regulation," and had the economic management feature of being "relaxed when delegated and stagnant when regulated." "Delegation" refers to the divesting of some powers of economic management by the central government to the local governments to fire up their enthusiasm. "Regulation" refers to the central government taking back the power delegated to the local governments to strengthen her control over the overall economy.

As the market-oriented reform deepens, decentralization reforms have also made great progress. From an economic standpoint, such decentralization reforms are mainly embodied in the following points:

Firstly, the authority on financial revenue and expenditure has shifted to the local governments. In the era of the planned economy, China adopted a system in which central and local financial revenue and expenditure were subject to unified regulation and management by the central government. As an important element of economic decentralization carried out during the reform and opening up, changes to the financial system was carried out three times in 1980, 1985, and 1988, respectively. This was done to achieve a system of "financial contracting" between the local and central governments. Various local governments established independent contractual relationships with the central government, whereby a certain proportion or amount of local revenue was transferred to the central treasury and the rest could be used by local governments at their own discretion. Although this institutional change aroused the enthusiasm of the local governments and promoted economic development, the central government's proportion of the total government revenue had been declining since the reform and opening up. The proportion further dropped to about 22% before the "tax revenue distribution system" was implemented in 1994, weakening the ability of the central government to control at the macro-level.

An affluent village in a coastal area of China.

Secondly, administrative authority of the state-owned enterprises was delegated. Before the reform and opening up, large and medium-sized SOEs were affiliated with various departments of the central government. In other words, they were managed along administrative lines of division. As the central government implemented the "decentralization of power and transfer of profits" reform for SOEs, affiliation and administrative authority of most SOEs were also transferred from the central government to local governments at various levels.

Thirdly, the central government gradually delegated most of her power for local economic development, with the aims of arousing their enthusiasm and enhancing the initiative of local governments in their economic development. This made it easier for local governments to better adapt to local conditions. In particular, local governments gained decision-making power regarding approval of investments in small and medium-sized projects, as well as the power to allocate materials and to engage in foreign trade.

These decentralization reforms significantly boosted the initiative of the local governments. As independent economic entities, the local governments played an important role in local economic development. However, sometimes the local governments executed policies of the central government, while at other times, they are acting out of their own interests. Since the interests of the local and central governments were not entirely similar, the relationship between the two governments was fraught with contradictions and conflicts.

The mobilization of the initiative of local governments is a significant factor in the success of China's reform and opening up. Following the implementation of decentralization reforms, the local governments have realized that economic development is closely related to their own interests, and have thus implemented the guidelines and policies of the central government more actively. In addition, the local governments played key roles in active innovation and courageous practice on the road of institutional changes designed by China.

For the sake of local interests, the local governments actively took part in the reform of SOEs, developed and supported the local economy's core industries, and actively cultivated their markets for products and factors of production. In addition, they took drastic measures to attract foreign direct investments, promote foreign trade and vigorously implemented various institutional changes according to the instructions of the central authorities.

The success of rural reform used to depend to a large extent on the local governments. The move by Anhui, Sichuan, and other areas to allow farmers' spontaneous acts of reform eventually resulted in a change of the agricultural production and management system that has been recognized by the central government. The restructuring of the SOE, reform on social security and rural tax and fees, were all led and experimented on by the local governments. This provided practical experience and a reform package for the central government. In the end, this package became an institutional change popularized throughout the country.

Without the central government's top-down incentives to local governments and their active grassroots support, it is impossible to successfully complete China's gradual reforms. It is the interaction between the central government and local governments that allowed China's reform to proceed without encountering excessive fluctuations. This interaction has enabled China's economy to achieve significant growth since reform and opening up began more than 30 years ago.

As a large country with such uneven economic development, China requires macroeconomic regulation and direct control by the central government. Therefore, the local governments cannot hold too much power because as stakeholders, they are not responsible for the overall balance of the national economy and may adopt some policies contrary to the guidelines of the central government in order to maximize their interests. For example, in seeking unduly high rate of GDP growth, they will resort to any schemes

In China, substantial disparities in economic development exist between the mid-western and eastern regions. This picture, taken in December 2007, shows the Tujia ethnic minorities in Wufeng, Hubei Province, finally getting access to safe and sanitary tap water.

for quick results and hence make excessive investments. From their point of view, such investments seem reasonable, but from a national perspective, such investments give rise to problems such as redundant construction and unreasonable policies.

In order to protect local businesses, local governments may practice a form of local protectionism by resorting to administrative measures. Such measures include the prohibition of the inflow of industrial products from other regions or restriction to the outflow of local agricultural and secondary products, raw materials, and energy resources. Such a "feudalistic" economic phenomenon of artificial market segmentation and protectionism is at odds with the central government's spirit of building a unified national market system.

In order to raise the level of financial revenue and expenditure of the central government, China implemented a reform of tax distribution in 1994. This reform redefined both the central and local governments' sources of revenue and level of tax burden. This move reversed the decline in the central government's revenue and improved her level of macroeconomic control and performance in providing public services throughout the country.

At the same time, the central government used a series of measures such as cross-regional exchange of provincial-level cadres to restore the capacity and authority of central finance to effectively eliminate the uncooperative behavior of "coming up with a countermeasure to whatever policies the central government introduces." The central government requires financial resources to improve the infrastructure of the ethnic minorities and economically backward areas through transfer payments in order to achieve coordinated development across different regions.

In 2001, the Chinese government put forward the "Develop the Western Region" strategy in order to promote economic development in the western inland areas and also narrow the economic development gap between the eastern coastal regions and western inland regions. Financial expenditures began to shift toward the west to increase efforts in investing and building infrastructure in the western regions, as well as to provide some other preferential policies. Results from the implementation of this strategy proved that the policies of the Chinese government have accelerated the economic development of China's western regions and effectively alleviated the development gap between the eastern and western regions.

The northeast region of China used to be her heavy industrial hub. Due to the difficulties during the transition period, economic development has been slow since the start of reform and opening up. In order to revitalize this heavy industrial hub in Northeast China, the Chinese government accelerated economic development through a series of policies that drew upon the government's increased fiscal capacity. Thereafter, the economic development of central China also came within the range of the central government's vision. Subsequently, it put forward the "Emergence of Central China" strategy.

The relationship between the central and local authorities is a major issue, especially so for a large country with uneven economic development. Efforts made at the beginning of the reform and opening up to utilize the initiative of local governments enabled the economy to achieve remarkable growth. As the level of economic development improves, the strengthening of the central government's fiscal capacity can also alleviate a series of problems including regional and income disparities. It can be seen that as conditions change, it is necessary to manage the relationship between central and local authorities carefully.

There are still many problems that need to be addressed before China's economy can achieve rapid and sustainable development. To resolve these problems, there needs to be positive interaction between the central and local governments. This involves dynamically adjusting the allocation of authority between the central and local governments as the economic system changes and the level of economic development improves. In this way, the governments can maximize their effectiveness.

A Hybrid Ownership Structure Dominated by Public Ownership

Ownership structure refers to the inter-relationship, position, and proportion of different forms of ownership related to the means of production in certain socioeconomic forms. The nature of ownership in dominant and leading positions determines the nature of the ownership structure of the society.

China's ownership structure has undergone dramatic changes. After 1949, China entered a neo-democratic economic society consisting of five economic sectors: a socialist state-operated economy, a semi-socialist cooperative economy, an individual economy of farmers and craftsmen, a private capitalist economy, and a state capitalist economy. From 1953 to 1956, the Chinese government completed the socialist transformation of individual farming, individual handicraft industry, and capitalist industry and commerce. Through the "Three Great Transformations," China basically abolished private ownership and achieved public ownership, moving China from a neo-democratic society to a socialist one. Individual farming and handicraft industries were transformed into a socialist collective economy, and the private capitalist economy was transformed into a socialist state-owned economy.

Traditional socialist theory holds that the elimination of private ownership is equivalent to achieving socialism. Therefore, influenced by both the Soviet model and the catching-up strategy of prioritizing development of heavy industries, China merely sought the "advanced nature" of the forms of ownership and engaged only in the "large, public, and pure" campaign.[1] China excluded, restricted, and attacked non-public sectors of the economy as "the rat's tail of capitalism" and single-mindedly took public ownership as the fundamental economic system.

Before the reform and opening up in 1978, the public sector was dominant in China's economy. There were only 140,000 individual operators employing 150,000 people and private economy and foreign capital nearly vanished into thin air. However, it has been proven that this type of ownership was detached from reality and at that time, China's overall level of productivity was low. Multilayered and unbalanced, the socialization of production remains at a low level, therefore constraining the development of productivity. In fact, the same ownership can be realized differently at different stages of the development of productive forces. There are different ways of realizing public ownership, which should include state ownership, collective ownership, cooperative systems, and shareholding cooperative systems. These are in addition to the elements of public ownership in various forms of a diversified ownership economy. All modes of operation and forms of organization that reflect the law of socialized production should be boldly utilized.

In the past, China mainly regarded the dominant position of public ownership as being superior in terms of quantity and structure. It was believed that the absolute quantity of the assets of the SOEs should account for a simple majority of the total assets in society. In addition, it was thought that the collective economy already in public ownership should be transferred to enterprises owned by the people at an accelerated pace.

At the 15th CPC National Congress held in 1997, the party made a theoretical breakthrough in the general understanding of "the dominant position of public ownership" regardless of regions, industries, and quality. Instead, the party noted that the dominant position of public ownership was mainly expressed through public assets being dominant in the total assets of society. The state-owned economy controlled the lifeline of the national economy and played a leading role in economic development. Also, some regions and industries may have some differences. To maintain the superiority of the large quantity of public assets, more attention should be paid on improving the quality of

---

[1]Namely, the goal of the socialist model promoted by the planned economy; this is achieved through "large" grassroots organizations such as the people's communes; high degree of "public" ownership; and "pure" economic composition of socialism.

these public assets. The leading role of the state-owned economy arises mainly from her ability to control the national economy. As long as the state controls the lifeline of the economy, the state-owned economy's control and competitiveness will be strengthened. Reductions in the proportion of state-owned economy in the national economy will not affect the overall socialist nature of China. The meaning of state-owned economy has also changed over time. In the past, the enterprises were state-owned and state-run, and had the rights of ownership and management. Now, the state has become the main stakeholder of these state-owned enterprises, which have diverse sources of investment and substantial social investments. In particular, listed SOEs have a large amount of foreign capital.

The formation process of China's basic economic system is also a process of the non-public sectors of the economy which has grown from being small and weak to large and strong. In the early 1980s, in order to resolve the unemployment problem in the cities and find a solution to the problem of surplus rural labor, China encouraged the development of the individual economy. However, she did not take into account the non-public sectors of the economy at the level of the basic socialist economy system and only "regarded the individual economy of the working people in certain areas as a necessary supplement to the public sector of the economy." As the reform and opening up progressed, the non-public sectors of the economy played an increasingly prominent role in areas such as promoting the growth of the national economy, expanding

After 30 years of development, the private economy has gradually become a major contributor to China's economic growth. This picture shows a cell phone production line of a private technology enterprise in China.

employment, invigorating the market, and improving people's lives. Accordingly, the Chinese government also began to recognize the necessity of the existence and development of the non-public sectors of the economy under the existing level of productivity. At her 12th CPC National Congress held in 1982, the party encouraged the individual economy to develop systematically within the limits prescribed by the state and industrial and commercial administration, so as to make it a necessary and useful supplement to the public sector of the economy.

Proceeding from the reality of the primary stage of socialism, the party noted at her 15th CPC National Congress in 1997 that all the non-public sectors of the economy are important components of the socialist market economy. In her report at the 16th CPC National Congress in 2002, the party summarized the practical experience of ownership reform. It was determined to unwaveringly consolidate and develop the public sector of the economy, and unwaveringly encourage, support, and guide the development of the non-public sectors of the economy. The party pointed out that "all sectors in the economy can exploit their respective advantages in market competition and stimulate one another for common development…instead of making them fight against one another; they can be incorporated into the process of the socialist modernization drive." In other words, the public sector and non-public sectors of the economy need to utilize their respective advantages in ownership, depend upon and complement each other. Both the public and non-public sectors of the economy should compete, promote, and interact with each other so that everyone benefits from the competition. The public and non-public sectors of the economy should commingle and blend into each other.

In her report to the 17th CPC National Congress in 2007, the party further proposed that "equal protection of property rights should be enforced, and hence create a new situation in which all economic sectors compete on an equal footing and complement each other," which reinforced the deep insight of the basic socialist economy system. China has also created and improved laws and regulations for promoting the development of the non-public sectors of the economy. She has improved the legal system for protecting private property.

In 1999, the National People's Congress amended the constitution for the third time to specify that "individual and private sectors of the economy operating within the limits prescribed by law are an important component of the socialist market economy." In 2004, the National People's Congress amended the constitution for the fourth time to recognize the legal status of lawful private property. In the following year, the State Council promulgated the *Opinions on Encouraging, Supporting, and Guiding the Development of Individual and Private Economy and Other Non-Public Sectors of the Economy*. In

2007, a series of laws were publicized related to advancing reforms of the public sector of the economy, and promoting the development of the non-public sectors of the economy including the Property Law, Enterprise Income Tax Law, Anti-Monopoly Law and Labor Contract Law.

In conclusion, based on China's understanding of the primary stage of socialism, she has finally established a basic economic system at the primary stage of socialism in which "public ownership is dominant and diverse forms of ownership develop together." As China develops, she will have a greater understanding of the issues concerning ownership structure, and will enrich and develop the theory of socialist market economy to guide China's practice of economic development.

A Distribution System with Equal Emphasis on Fairness and Efficiency

The distribution system is a major theoretical and practical issue. Distribution is an important link in the process of social reproduction that plays a crucial role in connecting production and consumption. It reveals the relationship of the interests between various economic stakeholders in certain social systems and reflects various determinants behind such relationships. Whether the distribution system is rational and effective has a direct bearing on sustainable, rapid, healthy, and steady development of the national economy. In addition, it concerns social stability, and the lasting stability and durable peace of the nation.

For 20 years since the completion of socialist transformation in 1956 to the reform and opening up, distribution according to work was the only mode of income distribution. Specifically, the wage system was implemented for enterprises, government departments, and institutions owned by the people and urban collectively-owned enterprises; the work point system was implemented for the rural collective economy. Its main features are listed as follows:

Firstly, the government held an absolutely dominant position in the income distribution system. An eight-grade wage scale system was implemented for urban enterprises owned by the Chinese people; the graded wage system was implemented for institutions including government agencies and institutions engaged in science, education, culture, and public health. The government specifically determined the wage standard of every industry and every wage category. In the rural areas, the government strictly determined the allocation principles, procedures and proportional relations between accumulation and consumption of the collective economy. The production team was the basic unit of collective operation (each production team had an average of 30 farming households). Farmers earned their work points according to the amount, intensity, and strength of the labor delivered, and participated in distribution of the production team's income based on the work points they earned. The value of work points depended on the production team's income. The production team's net income depended on the quantity and price of agricultural products, and the prices of agricultural products were mostly set, planned, and managed by the state, so the income level of farmers was also subject to the regulation of national price plans.

Secondly, significant egalitarianism existed. The wage levels and standards of the same department and industry were basically uniform nationwide (with small regional differences). Meanwhile, the wages of the employees in enterprises had nothing to do with its operating conditions and economic efficiency. As long as the wage levels of enterprises were the same, regardless of whether the enterprise yielded good economic returns or made a loss, employees in different enterprises would receive the same wages. In the rural collective economy, farmers received assignments from production teams and worked collectively. Grain and other necessities of life were allocated based on work points and on a per capita basis, so the same significant propensity toward equal distribution existed in the rural areas.

China encourages her citizens to earn multiple streams of income.

Since her reform and opening up, China has conducted a series of specific reforms in the field of distribution to motivate people toward high productivity, with a strong focus on overcoming the significant egalitarianism in the old income distribution system. In 1978, Deng Xiaoping first proposed that "some workers and farmers in some areas and businesses should be allowed to earn more income and live a better life due to their diligence and higher achievements."

Reform of the distribution system started initially alongside the implementation of the household contract responsibility system in the rural areas in the early 1980s. The household contract responsibility system drew a clear distinction between the rights, responsibilities, and interests of the state, collectives, and individuals. This system most effectively linked farmers' income with the fruits of their labor. The success of distribution reform in rural areas has had a far-reaching impact on the later reform of China's distribution system.

The Third Plenary Session of the 12th CCCPC held in 1984 proposed that enterprises could decide on employee bonuses at their own discretion based on their operating conditions, and that the state would only impose an appropriate tax on the above-norm bonus on enterprises. Within enterprises, the difference between the wages of various jobs had to be widened to fully reflect the principle of rewarding the diligent and punishing the lazy. In addition, it should fully demonstrate the income differences between intellectual and physical work, complex and simple, skilled and unskilled, as well as heavy physical and light physical labor. At the same time, the practice of low pay for intellectual work should be changed.

In January 1985, the State Council released the *Circular Concerning the Wage Reform of State-Owned Enterprises*. It decided to implement a method of floating the total payroll in proportion to the economic efficiency in large and medium-sized SOEs, starting from 1985. As the theory of the primary stage of socialism was better understood, the 13th CPC National Congress proposed that income distribution should be made mainly according to work done and supplemented by various other modes of distribution, including legitimate non-labor based income. Furthermore, distribution policies should not only help successful enterprises and honest workers become better off first, but also prevent the polarization of the rich and the poor. In addition, policies should raise efficiency while adhere to the direction of common prosperity and embody social justice.

The 14th CPC National Congress in 1992 explicitly proposed the establishment of a socialist market economy system, which brought the reform of the distribution system onto the correct path that followed the tenets of macroeconomic theory and also conformed to China's national conditions. The 14th CPC National Congress proposed that the distribution system should mainly consist of distribution according to work and be supplemented by other modes of distributions, at the same time taking into account both efficiency and equity. The report of the 15th CPC National Congress specifically proposed allowing and encouraging capital, technology, and other production factors to participate in income distribution. It also proposed that the distribution system according to work done and the distribution system according to production factors should be combined, thus clarifying the position of distribution according to production factors. At the same time, it proposed that the distribution structure be improved by giving higher priority to efficiency in order to promote economic development, as well as giving consideration to equity in order to promote social stability.

For the theory of distribution, the 16th CPC National Congress in 2002 clearly defined distribution according to production factors. The congress also pointed out how the principle of "emphasizing efficiency in primary distribution while maintaining equity in redistribution" can be implemented. Firstly, the principle defined labor, capital, technology, and management as basic production factors, without denying the active role of production factors including knowledge, resources, and information in wealth creation. Secondly, it specified the distribution of production factors according to contribution. Thirdly, it provided a clear answer on the relationship between efficiency and equity, namely "emphasize efficiency, allow the market to exert its role and encourage a part of the population to become better off first through honest labor and lawful operations in primary distribution; emphasize equity, strengthen the government's function of regulating income distribution, and adjust income gaps that become too wide."

In conclusion, China's distribution system has undergone the following processes of change: the evolutionary development from a distribution system based on work done to the current system based on production factors; the evolutionary development from giving priority to equity to the current priority on efficiency while paying attention to equity too; and to the current emphasis on both equity and efficiency.

Coordinated Urban and Rural Development

The relationship between urban and rural areas is an important issue that has to be dealt with, as a result of China's industrialization, urbanization, and modernization. Viewed from an economic perspective, the relationship between urban and rural areas is synonymous with that of industry and agriculture. Solving any problems regarding the relationship between urban and rural areas is, in a way, correctly handling problems concerning coordinated development of industry and agriculture.

After the founding of the People's Republic of China, along with the restoration of the national economy, industrialization became the top priority in building the entire national economy. Centered on this goal, the relationship between urban and rural areas entailed efforts to address two issues. Firstly, how to accumulate funds for industrialization and accelerate agricultural development to solve the problem of feeding the vast Chinese population despite limited farmland. Secondly, how to coordinate the relationship between urban and rural areas (the relationship between industry and agriculture) under the strategy of giving priority to the development of heavy industries to maintain social stability under the condition of a low rate of consumption, and ensure that China's industrialization is reached as soon as possible.

The method adopted at that time was to pursue a path of agricultural cooperative movement that had three main objectives:

(1) transform the backward small-peasant economy to enable significant agricultural development;

(2) ensure necessary capital accumulation for industrialization; and

(3) maintain social stability and avoid polarization in the process of industrialization and a high rate of accumulation.

China has entered the phase of the "industry nurturing agriculture." This farmer from Lixian County, Gansu Province, shows the "benefits" of the new agricultural policies.

However, after complete socialist transformation with objectives of a singular public ownership and a planned economy, the superiority of the socialist economy as originally imagined did not appear. Even for the relationship between urban and rural areas, the food scarcity problem persisted and the agricultural surplus for industrialization was very limited. So, the state continued to tighten her control of the rural economy, not only preventing the development of diversified agriculture in rural areas, but also restricting the migration of the rural population into the cities. There was even a reverse migration of the urban population to rural areas (e.g., educated urban youths going to the countryside during the Cultural Revolution for 1966–1976). As a consequence, the urbanization process was very slow.

After nearly 30 years of development after 1949, China has made significant progress in promoting the use of advanced technologies; electricity, fertilizers, pesticides, as well as irrigation and water conservation projects. However, due to the effects of the 10-year Cultural Revolution and enfettered by "leftist" political views, agriculture and rural areas were still confined to the planned economy system and farmers were still confined to a backward countryside away from the urban areas.

Prior to 1978, the collective operating system that integrated government administration and economic management limited the motivation of farmers' productivity. Hence, the farming of grain and other major agricultural products could not always meet the needs of population growth. Both urban and rural residents led an impoverished life, as the problem of feeding and clothing the Chinese people throughout the country had not been resolved and 250 million farmers lived below the poverty line. In the cities, the problem of unemployment became increasingly serious and the policy of sending a large number of educated urban youths to rural areas caused discontent among urban residents, especially the youths. This policy was not only difficult to sustain, but also became a major problem that threatened social stability. The relationship between the urban and rural areas reached an important turning point.

Before reform and opening up, the revenue support received from farmers and the rural areas came mainly from agricultural taxes and low-priced farm and secondary products (through state monopoly over the sales and purchase and the wide gap in prices between rural and urban areas). In other words, the countryside accumulated funds and reduced the cost of industrialization by providing agricultural surpluses to the cities. Meanwhile, the state reduced the pressure on cities and maintained social stability by limiting the movement of farmers. Some of the rural population was transferred to cities through school admissions, military enlistments, and planned recruitments, but the number of people transferred was very limited.

After reform and opening up, the way in which farmers and the rural areas supported industrialization and the cities underwent tremendous changes. Along with the abolition of the system of "state monopoly over sales and purchase" of agricultural products and the general adoption of market principles for agricultural products, the proportion of revenue from rural areas that supported industrialization and urban cities through direct and indirect agricultural surplus became increasingly low. Meanwhile, support for industrialization through the supply of cheap labor by farmers and rural resources (capital and land) increasingly became the main form of support.

Firstly, the large amount of cheap labor supplied by farmers provided abundant and affordable human resources for economic development since the reform and opening up, which also greatly reduced the cost of industrialization and thus increased the rate of enterprises' capital accumulation. In particular, it provided rapidly growing capital accumulation for export-oriented enterprises and labor-intensive enterprises.

Secondly, since the reform and opening up, farmers have provided low-valued land and real estate for urban development, economic development zones and a large number of infrastructure projects such as transportation. In addition, many cities have acquired significant land revenue funds through compulsory purchases of farmers' land to close the gap of funding urban development budgets. This method is commonly known as an "enterprise type" of urban development.

Thirdly, farmers inject large amounts of rural funds into cities and towns by promoting the development of small towns through township enterprises and directly making investment in cities.

The three above-mentioned phenomena—where the rural areas provide support for the industrialization and urbanization of cities—have been the major driving forces behind China's rapid economic growth since 1978, particularly for the extraordinary growth in foreign trade and rapid expansion of urban space.

Furthermore, the rapid increase in the supply of agricultural products after 1978 not only served as a prerequisite for the "sudden rise" of township enterprises, but also enabled the state to guarantee the low prices of farm and secondary products and the stability of consumer prices for daily necessities, following the market-oriented reform that revoked grain and oil subsidies for cities.

In promoting the rapid development of the national economy, the rate of urbanization had increased and thus brought about prosperity to the entire country. This change in the relationship between urban and rural areas after the reform and opening up had widened the development and income gaps between the two areas even though the gaps were actually briefly narrowed in the early 1980s. If some implicit benefits and privileges of urban residents are converted into cash, the income gap between urban and rural residents may

More rural residents have become urban residents after the reform of the household registration system.

reach a ratio of 6:1. Obviously, such an increase in disparity is inconsistent with the national goal of common prosperity.

As China's economy developed and grew, the state had the financial resources to change the relationship between urban and rural areas from one where agriculture subsidized industries and the rural areas supported cities to a new relationship in which the industry subsidized agriculture and cities supported the development of the rural areas.

The 16th CPC National Congress in 2002 brought the understanding of the relationship between urban and rural areas to a new height. The congress noted that to solve the "agriculture, the countryside, and farmer" problems, the traditional limitation of considering agriculture, the countryside, and farmers disjointedly must be overcome, and all the while keeping in mind the overall situation of economic development for society.

At the Third Session of the 10th National People's Congress in March 2004, Premier Wen Jiabao of the State Council put forward a plan for gradually revoking agricultural taxes within five years and increasing the state's fiscal expenditure on primary education in rural areas. At the Central Economic Working Conference held in December the same year, General Secretary of the CCCPC Hu Jintao stressed that: "China as a whole has entered the phase of promoting agriculture with industry and increasing development of the rural areas with the support of cities. We should adapt ourselves to this trend by adjusting the national income distribution pattern more consciously and actively support "agriculture, the countryside, and farmer" development.

Based on a better understanding of the relationship between industry and agriculture and between urban and rural areas, the Chinese government made a major, historic re-adjustment to the relationship between the two areas in 2005. In March 2005, Premier Wen Jiabao further proposed that industry and cities must support agriculture and the rural areas. At a press conference held on March 14, 2005, he stated that: "We have entered the second stage... the second stage is the implementation of the policy of cities supporting the rural areas and industry subsidizing agriculture by 'giving more to, taking less from, and relaxing control over' the farmers." From 2003 to 2007, government spending on "agriculture, the countryside, and farmer" programs reached RMB 1.6 trillion, 10 times the amount spent during 1950–1978 before reform and opening up and 1.3 times as much as that during 1979–2002. The central government injected RMB 595.5 billion into "agriculture, the countryside, and farmer" programs in 2008, an increase of RMB 163.7 billion or 37.9% compared to the previous year. The amount of direct subsidies for grain farmers, comprehensive subsidies for means of agricultural production, subsidies for superior crop varieties, and subsidies for the purchase of farm machinery reached RMB 103 billion, twice as much as that of 2007. The minimum purchase price for grain was increased substantially three times, with the total increase exceeding 20%. In 2009, in order to lessen the impact of the world financial crisis on Chinese farmers' income and the rural economy, the central government budgeted to spend RMB 716.1 billion on "agriculture, the countryside, and farmer" programs, up from RMB 120.6 billion or 20.25% from 2008.

As shown by China's full-scale effort to let industries subsidize agriculture and encourage cities to support the rural areas by building a new socialist countryside, the industry–agriculture relationship and that between urban and rural areas in China have entered a new and historic phase of development. However, it should also be noted that China's industrialization, urbanization, and agricultural modernization still have a long way to go and will be subject to more severe resource and environmental constraints than in the past 30 years. Nonetheless, China will remain committed to balancing urban and rural development through altering government's conceptions, transfer payments from state coffers, and economic development.

Equal and Mutually Beneficial Foreign Economic Relations

Internal reform and opening up are the two jet engines that that drive China's economic growth. In the past, China strove for survival in an environment of external economic blockade. However, modern China now has closer ties with the rest of the world.

At the beginning of her reform and opening up, China's foreign trade was seen as a way to supplement expanded socialist reproduction. It was limited to mutual exchange of essential goods and also regulated supply and demand. Trade was subjected to highly-centralized, mandatory and planned management by the state-owned foreign trade enterprises. As a result, foreign trade was far from being adaptive to the needs of economic development.

After her reform and opening up, China changed this highly centralized foreign trade management system by adding more foreign trade ports and decentralizing foreign trade management rights. The government promoted exports through effective policies such as tax reimbursement for exports and regulated foreign trade through economic means such as prices, exchange rates, interest rates, tax rebates, and export credits. Meanwhile, by setting up SEZs and opening up the strategic coastal areas, China's development and export-oriented economy achieved a major breakthrough. Her exports rose from 26th place in the world rankings in 1980 to 14th in 1989.

In order to attract foreign direct investments, the Law of the People's Republic of China on Chinese–Foreign Equity Joint Ventures was promulgated in 1979. China approved the first three foreign-invested enterprises in 1980. In 1986, the State Council promulgated the Regulations on Encouraging Foreign Investment. Since then, China has implemented several preferential policies for attracting foreign investments to SEZs, coastal open trade cities and coastal open economic zones. These policies included: expanding local authorities' power in approving foreign investments to encourage various cities to take the initiative of attracting foreign investments; improving the investment environment; and other developments that promoted and attracted foreign investments.

In the 1990s, China established a unitary and well-managed floating exchange rate system, implemented a bank exchange settlement and sales system, and canceled foreign exchange retention. The mandatory import and export plan was canceled and public bidding for quotas of some export commodities was implemented. The gradual decentralization of foreign trade management rights prompted the transition from the examination and approval system to the registration system. China also actively transformed her foreign trade enterprises' operating models and carried out shareholding system pilot programs. The policy of tax reimbursement for exports was improved and the development of foreign trade through export credit, export credit insurance, and other common international practices were supported.

At the same time, an all-rounded, multi-level and wide-ranging pattern of opening up was taking shape. In 1990, the central government decided to develop and open up Pudong New Area in Shanghai. In 1992, the government extended outwards the boundaries of opened-up regions and successively

An increasing number of foreign enterprises are now closely linked to China's economy.

opened up six port cities along the Yangtze River including Chongqing, Wuhan, and Jiujiang, 13 land-locked cities including Manchuria and all inland provincial cities, and implemented flexible regional economic policies that encouraged foreign investments. In the subsequent years, the government also opened up a large number of eligible inland cities and counties.

In the 1990s, based on the dynamic local and international situations, the Chinese government successively proposed strategies such as "win through quality," "market diversification," "increase trade," and "invigorate trade through science and technology." China's foreign trade made a second leap forward. Her exports grew at an annual rate of 14% from 1990 to 1999. By 1999, China had jumped to ninth place in the world rankings.

In 1999, according to the changes and development in local and international scenarios, the central government put forward the "overseas business expansion" strategy. It called on all localities and departments to work together to accelerate the establishment of the marketing, guarantee, regulatory, and services systems for the overall "overseas business expansion" strategy. The government also promoted the development of overseas investments in factories, processing and assembling enterprises, overseas resource development, foreign project contracting, and labor service cooperation.

In 2001, with China's accession to the WTO, her opening up entered a new phase:

- from opening up within a limited scope, fields and regions to all-rounded, multi-level and wide-ranging opening up;
- from policy-based opening up characterized by pilot efforts to institutional opening-up within the legal framework;

- from mainly unilateral self-initiated opening up of markets to bilateral opening up of markets between China and WTO members;
- from opening up in which China passively accepts international economic and trade rules to opening up in which China actively participates in drawing up international economic and trade rules;
- from opening up in which economies and trades are coordinated only through bilateral consultation mechanisms to opening up in which multilateral and bilateral mechanisms are integrated with and promote each other.

Accession to the WTO opened up new avenues for China's participation in economic globalization and paved the way for the development of the national economy and society. Since her accession to the WTO, China has opened up many service areas as promised, such as finance, telecommunications, construction, distribution, law, tourism, and transportation. More than 3,000 laws, administrative regulations, and departmental rules have been developed, amended, and repealed; intellectual property protection has been strengthened and the investment environment has been further improved. The scale of utilization of foreign capital has been expanding, making China the first among other developing countries for 15 consecutive years, with the average amount of foreign capital in actual use reaching nearly US$59 billion each year. From 2000 to 2007, foreign trade grew rapidly at an annual average rate of 24.3%. China's total foreign trade volume reached US$2.5616 trillion in 2008, making China the world's third largest trading nation. This marks China's economic connectivity to the rest of the world.

Chapter 4

China's Economic Development: Standards and Achievements

For 60 years since the founding of the People's Republic of China, through trial and error, she has gradually discovered a development path suitable for China's own characteristics. Her achievements in economic development are enormous, as manifested by the continuous growth of the aggregate economic volume, rising per capita output, continuous improvement in education and health standards, substantial increase in population, rising level of urbanization, and continuous improvement in the Chinese people's living standards.

Rapid Growth of the National Economy

China's GDP grew from RMB 67.9 billion in 1952 to RMB 31.4045 trillion in 2008, passing the RMB 30-trillion mark with an increase of 9.6% over 2007. Her per capita GDP has also grown from RMB 118 in 1952 to RMB 22,698 in 2008. Both China's aggregate economic volume and per capita GDP have seen tremendous increases in the past 60 years. Based on the December 1, 2009, exchange rate of RMB 6.8271 to US$1, China's per capita GDP has crossed the US$3,000 mark. In 2008, China became the world's third-largest economy (and third highest GDP in the world) after the United States and Japan, and is expected to exceed Japan to become the second largest economy in the world in 2010.

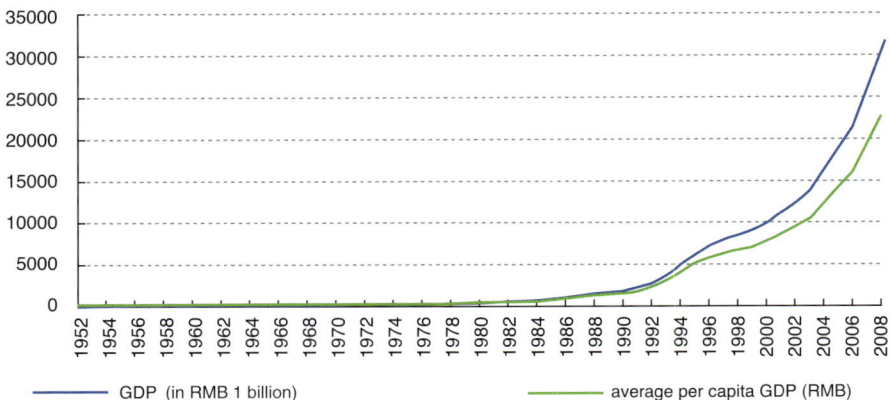

Source: *China Statistics Yearbook (1952–2008),* China National Bureau of Statistics.

China's GDP and average per capita GDP (1952–2008).

China's GDP grew at a rather uneven pace before the reform and opening up, due to the economic growth model of China's planned economy. Large-scale investment may foreshadow the need for further economic adjustment. China's GDP saw a significant decline during a period of national economic difficulties between 1959 and 1961. The economy also experienced negative growth during the Cultural Revolution (1966–1976). After the reform and opening up, China's economy became less volatile, despite the existence of economic cycles. China's GDP growth reached a low point during the 1997 Asian financial crisis, but the growth rate gradually climbed up again.

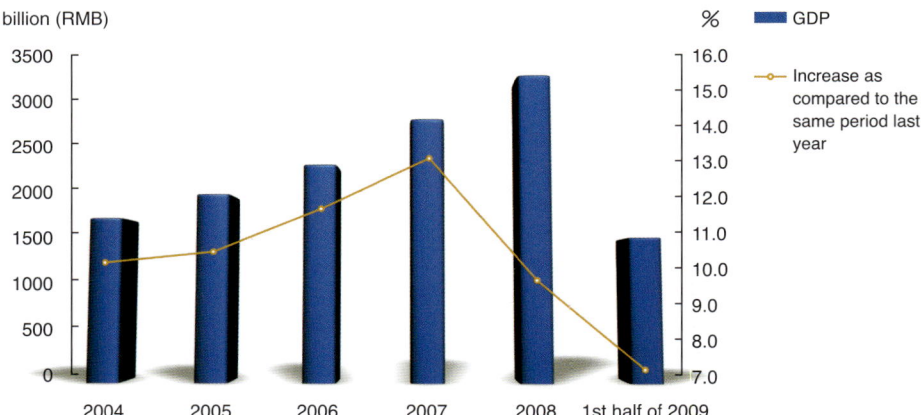

Source: *Statistical Bulletin of National Social and Economic Development in 2008 of People's Republic of China,* China National Bureau of Statistics.

China's GDP and her rate of increase between 2004 and the first half of 2009.

China's GDP growth rate has been above 10% in recent years. Rapid growth had guaranteed the steady and rapid increase in China's total GDP and per capita GDP.

Along with the rapid growth of China's GDP, output of both major agricultural and industrial products increased significantly. In 2008, China's gross grain output reached 528.5 million tons. Both the gross output and yield per unit hit a record high and grew for five consecutive years. The quantity of aquatic products and dairy products surpassed 47 million tons and 36 million tons, respectively. Successive annual increases in grain yields were attributed to both good climatic conditions for grain production and strong government policy support. In 2008, the Chinese government further enhanced her policy of strengthening agriculture and benefiting farmers. The output of main industrial products also greatly increased. In the same year, the raw coal output was close to 2.8 billion tons and crude oil output reached 190 million tons. The output of many industrial products was ranked first in the world.

Output of major agricultural products in China (1978–2008)						
Major Agricultural Products (10,000 tons)	1978	1990	2000	2006	2007	2008
Grain	30,476.5	44,624.3	46,217.5	49,804.2	50,160.3	52,871.0
Cotton	216.7	450.8	441.7	753.3	762.4	749.2
Oil Plants	521.8	1613.2	2954.8	2640.3	2568.7	2952.8
Sugar Cane	2111.6	5762.0	6828.0	9709.2	11,295.1	12,415.2
Sugar Beets	270.2	1452.5	807.3	750.8	893.1	1004.4
Tea	26.8	54.0	68.3	102.8	116.5	125.8
Fruits	657.0	1874.4	6225.1	17,102.0	18,136.3	19,220.2
Meat			6013.9	7089.0	6865.7	7278.7
Milk			919.1	3302.5	3633.4	3781.5
Aquatic Products	465.4	1237.0	3706.2	4583.6	4747.5	4894.9

Source: *China Statistics Yearbook 2008* and *Statistical Bulletin of National Social and Economic Development in 2008 of PRC*, China National Bureau of Statistics.

Output of industrial products in China (1978–2008)

Major Industrial Products	1978	1990	2000	2006	2007	2008
Textiles (100 million meters)	110	189	277	599	675	710
Sugar (10,000 tons)	227	582	700	949	1271	1449.5
Home Refrigerator (10,000 sets)	2.8	463	1279	3531	4397	4756.9
Air Conditioner (10,000 sets)	0.02	24	1827	6849	8014	8230.9
Washing Machine (10,000 sets)	0.04	663	1443	3561	4005	-NA-
Color TV (10,000 sets)	0.38	1033	3936	8375	8478	9033.1
Coal (100 million tons)	6.18	10.80	12.99	23.73	25.26	27.93
Crude Oil (10,000 tons)	10,405	13,831	16,300	18,477	18,632	19,000
Natural Gas (100 million cubic meters)	137.3	153.0	272.0	585.5	692.4	760.8
Electricity (100 million KW per hour)	2566	6212	13,556	28,657	32,816	34,668.8
Crude Steel (10,000 tons)	3178	6635	12,850	41,915	48,929	50,091.5
Steel Products (10, 000 tons)	2208	5153	13,146	46,893	56,561	58,488.1
Cement (10,000 tons)	6524	20,971	59,700	123,676	136,117	140,000

Source: China Statistics Yearbook (2008) and *Statistical Bulletin of National Social and Economic Development in 2008 of People's Republic of China,* China National Bureau of Statistics.

Price Stability

Along with China's economic growth, China's consumer price index (CPI) is also changing. Before the reform and opening up—with the exception of the period of national economic difficulties from 1959 to 1961 when there were substantial fluctuations—prices of goods were stable and the CPI did not fluctuate too much in the planned economy. In the planned economy, prices were not determined by market supply and demand, but rather by the government.

After the reform and opening up, prices fluctuated along with changes in supply and demand in the market. Four bouts of rather significant inflation have occurred. The first round occurred in the early 1980s, caused mainly by excessive growth in investments and a large increase in fiscal spending at the beginning of the reform and opening up. The second round occurred between 1984 and 1985 when overinvestment in fixed assets led to excessive total social demand, wage income increased at a rate faster than the increase in labor productivity, an increase in production costs, which finally resulted in costs pressure. As the scale of infrastructure construction, consumer demand, money supply and credit expanded rapidly, the economy overheated, intensifying inflation.

In the late 1980s, the third round of inflation happened due to the premature 1986 relaxation of the central government's 1984–1985 deflation policy, which resulted in serious demand inflation. During this period, the retail price index in 1988 hit a record high of 60 years since the founding of the People's Republic of China, with price increases and panic buying triggering a series of social problems. The fourth round happened during 1993–1995 when China's economy got onto the highway of rapid growth after the speech made by Deng Xiaoping during his tour of South China. This was largely caused by excessive expansion of FAI and continuing financial chaos. After three years of governance, China achieved an economic "soft landing" in 1996. In the twenty-first century, as the world economy recovers, China's economy has been showing favorable trends of high growth and low inflation.

The three major driving forces behind China's economic growth are investment, consumption, and net exports. In 1978, the scale of both investment and consumption was small and net exports still measured a negative US$1.14 billion. In the twenty-first century, the final consumption expenditure, gross capital accumulated and net exports of goods and services have all increased substantially. In 2008, these values have reached

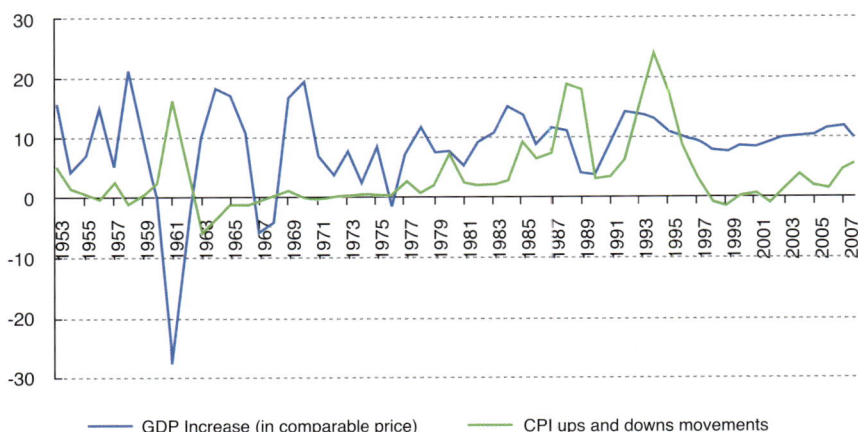

Source: *China Statistics Yearbook (1963–2007)* and *China Statistics Summary (2009)*, China National Bureau of Statistics.

China's GDP increases vs. CPI changes (1953–2008).

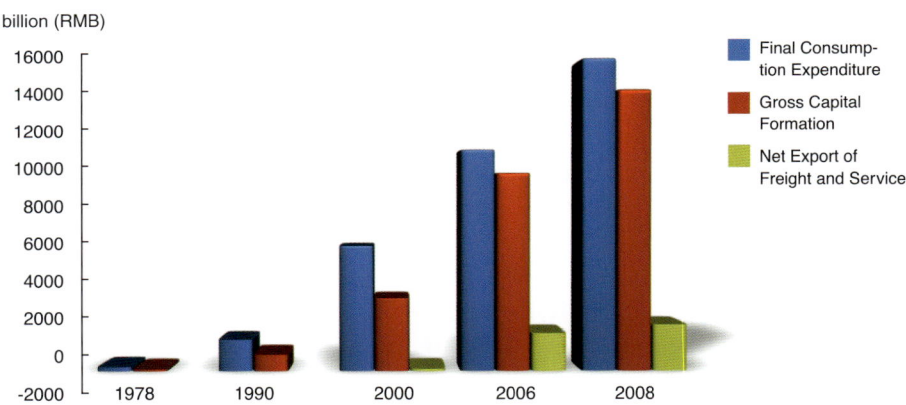

Source: *China Statistics Summary (2009)*, China National Bureau of Statistics.

Economic increases related to consumption, investment, and net exports (1978–2008).

RMB 14.91126 trillion, RMB 13.36123 trillion, and RMB 2.41349 trillion, respectively, in 2008.

China's FAI has been increasing in recent years. It was RMB 7.0477 trillion in 2004 and reached RMB 17.2291 trillion in 2008. The growth rate of FAI has also increased, and was 24.8% in 2007 and increased further to 25.5% in 2008.

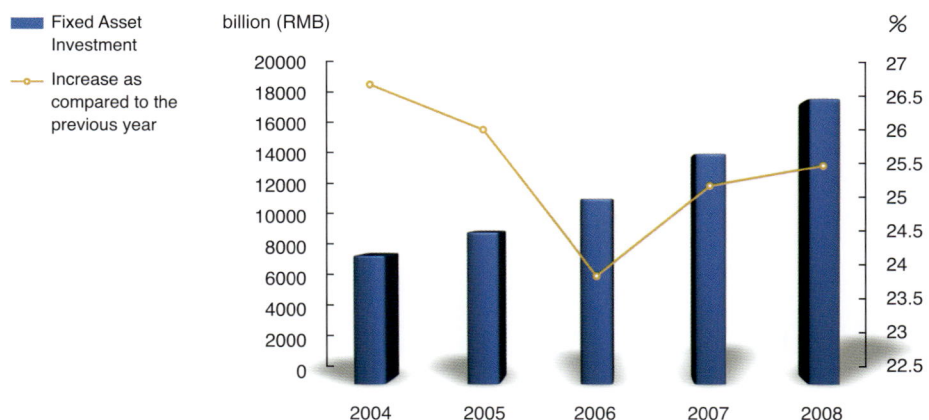

Source: *Statistical Bulletin of the National Social and Economic Development in 2008 of People's Republic of China,* China National Bureau of Statistics.

Increase of fixed asset investment in China (2004–2008).

An Evolving Industrial Structure

In the past 60 years of economic development, China's industrial structure as a whole has shown improvements. The proportion accounted for by the primary industry has been declining and its proportion of GDP has declined from 50% in 1952 to a little more than 10% in 2008. During the Great Leap Forward period, the proportion of GDP that agriculture accounted for declined abnormally but later rebounded. The proportion that the secondary industry accounted for has been showing an upward trend and rose from a little more than 20% in 1952 to less than 50% in 2008. The proportion fluctuated along with the overheating and adjustment of China's economy. During the Great Leap Forward period, the tertiary industry's proportion of GDP increased abnormally but also returned to normal later. There were more fluctuations in the tertiary industry's GDP in the subsequent years. In 1978, prior to reform and opening up, the tertiary industry's GDP share decreased annually as a result of China's large-scale investments in industry. After the reform and opening up, the GDP share increased on an annual basis and grew from around 20% in the early 1980s to 40% in 2008. China's industrial structure has undergone tremendous changes over the past 60 years; it has completed the first stage of transformation (from agriculture to industry) and will enter the second stage of transformation (from industry to services).

For China's industrial structure, the rate of contribution of the primary industry to overall GDP growth has been declining since the 1990s and only

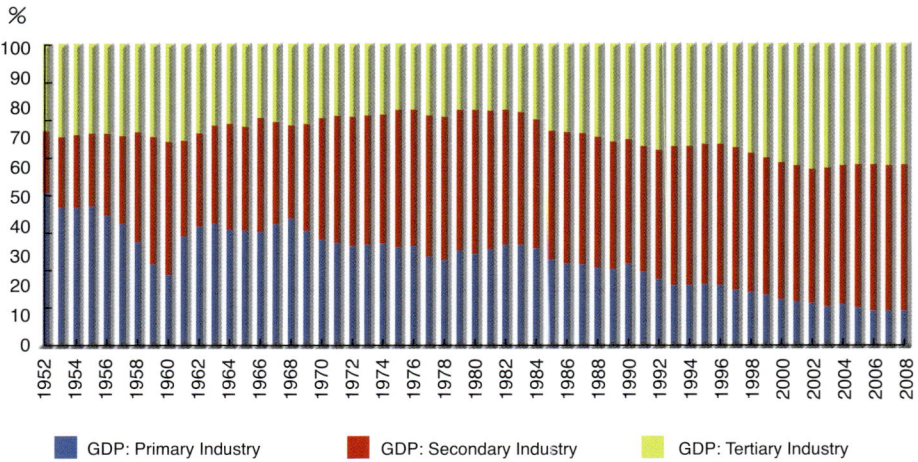

Source: *China Statistics Yearbook (1952–2008)*, China National Bureau of Statistics.

Improvements in China's industrial structure (1952–2008).

rose momentarily in 2004 due to the implementation of the Chinese government's policies for supporting agriculture and assisting farmers. The rate of contribution of the secondary industry to overall GDP growth has also been declining and only the rate of contribution of tertiary industry to overall GDP growth has been increasing annually. In 2008, the contribution rate to

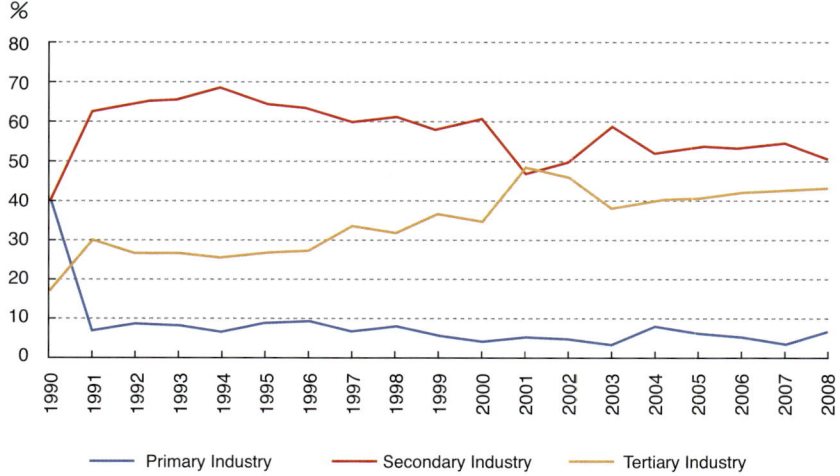

Source: *China Statistics Yearbook (1990–2008)* and *China Statistics Summary (2009)*, China National Bureau of Statistics.

China's industrial contributions to GDP increases (1990–2008).

GDP growth of the primary industry was 6.5%, while that of the secondary industry was 50.6%, and the tertiary industry was at 42.9%.

During the 1990s, the role of the primary industry in stimulating GDP growth has been diminishing, whereas the role of the tertiary industry in stimulating GDP growth has increased. The role of the secondary industry in stimulating GDP growth diminished during the mid- to late-1990s and has been fluctuating ever since then. Presently, the secondary industry remains the main driving force, especially the industrial sector within it. China has become a major manufacturing country, earning herself the nickname of the "world's factory." As China's economy develops and her industrial structure improves, the role of the tertiary industry in stimulating GDP growth is bound to surpass that of the secondary industry.

Gradual Improvements of the Employment Structure and Standards

Since the 1978's reform and opening up, China's employment structure has gone through significant changes. The employment rate in primary industry has been declining annually and it has dropped from 70.5% in 1978 to 39.6% in 2008. On the other hand, the employment rate in secondary industry has been increasing annually and it has increased from 17.3% in 1978 to 27.2% in 2008. The employment rate in tertiary industry has also been increasing at a pace faster than secondary industry, with its rate rising from 12.2% in 1978 to 33.2% in 2008.

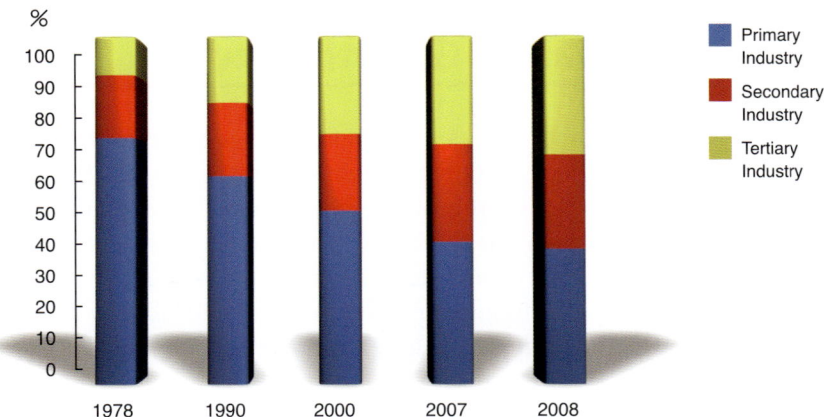

Source: *China Statistics Yearbook (1978–2008)* and *China Statistics Summary (2009)*, China National Bureau of Statistics.

Changes in China's employment structure (1978–2008).

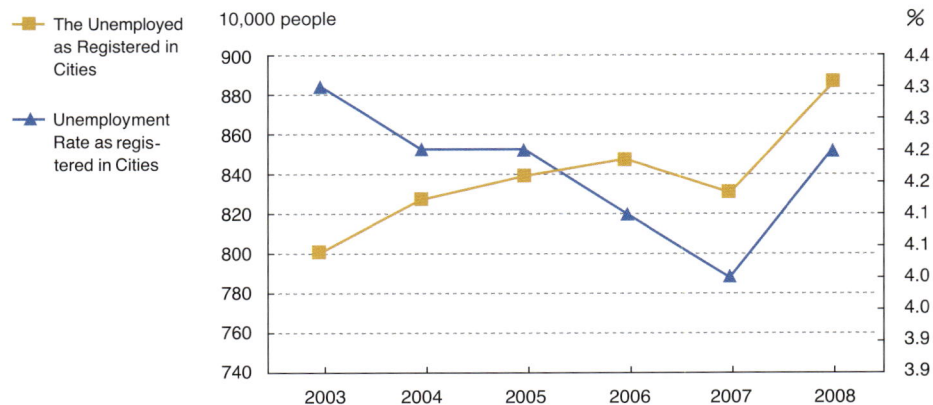

Source: *China Statistics Yearbook (2003–2008)* and *China Statistics Summary (2009)*, China National Bureau of Statistics.

Unemployment in China's cities (2003–2008).

Because China is a populous country in the middle-to-late stages of industrialization, increasing urban employment has always been the government's priority. As China's economy grows, the number of registered urban unemployed persons increased from 8 million in 2003 to 8.47 million in 2006, but declined to 8.3 million in 2007. In recent years, the registered urban unemployment rate has been declining annually, dropping from 4.3% in 2003 to 4% in 2007. This reflects the Chinese government's efforts to solve her unemployment issue.

Decline in Population Growth Rate

After 60 years of development, China's total population grew from 540 million in 1949 to 1.3 billion in 2008. Except for a slight decline in the late 1950s and early 1960s, the population has been growing continuously. As a result of China's birth-control policies and a change in her people's views on child-rearing brought about by the improved economic development, China's natural population growth rate has been declining annually since the mid- to late-1980s. In 2008, China's natural population growth rate dropped to 5.08%, which is only one-sixth of her 1957 peak of 29%.

The aging trend in China's population structure is evident. As the birth rate declines year by year, the proportion of the population over 60 years of age has been increasing annually and rose to 12% in 2008. The proportion of the total population aged 65 years and above has reached 8.3%. On the one hand, this

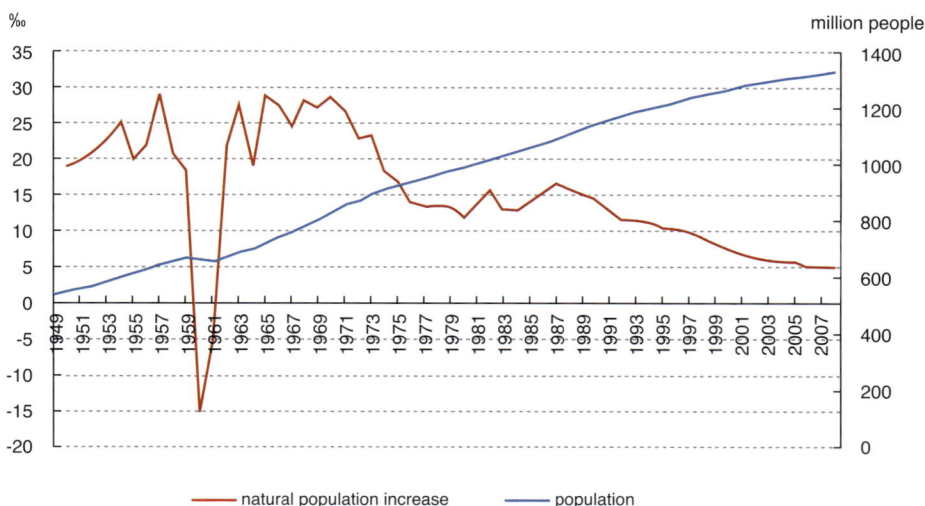

China's total population and her population growth (1949–2008).

is attributed to a reduction in fertility, on the other hand, this is also due to an increase in the life expectancy of the population[1]. The proportion of the population below the age of 20 has been declining annually and it decreased from nearly 40% in 1989 to around 26% in 2007. In the first several decades since the founding of the People's Republic of China, the number of children (≤14 years old) increased at a fast rate and accounted for 40% of the total population in the late 1960s. This trend of rapid growth has changed since the reform and opening up. Due to a low birth rate that led to a decline in the number of children, China's labor force will gradually decrease in the future and is predicted to drop to a level of below 60% by 2030. As China's economy develops, China will eventually join the ranks of "aged societies."

Improvements in the Standards of Education and Health Care

China's educational level was at a low level when the People's Republic of China was founded in 1949. Approximately 80% of the population was illiterate and the percentage of children who enrolled for school was only 20%. Right after

[1]The Chinese people's average life expectancy was only 42 years in 1950, however it reached 71.4 years in 2000 and increased to 73 years in 2008.

her founding, China gave high priority to improving the educational system. The state set up the Ministry of Education and an educational system that included primary, secondary, and tertiary institutions. At the same time, it also provided vocational and adult education. During the Cultural Revolution (1966–1976), the tertiary educational system was temporarily destroyed and universities stopped enrolment. Later, the tertiary education recommendation system was implemented, where suitable candidates were chosen from workers, farmers, and soldiers based on a set of political criteria. After the reform and opening up, China resumed the college entrance examination system. China's efforts at improving the educational system have been developing rapidly since then.

Firstly, the Chinese people have more opportunities to receive higher education and the level of education received has been raised annually. The proportion of students of the total population has been increasing and rose from 4.8% in 1949 to 18.2% in 2006. At the beginning of the twenty-first century, the number of university students increased rapidly, while the number of primary school students decreased. In 2008, for every 10,000 people, there were 204.2 university students, 766.7 secondary school students, and 781.9 primary school students.

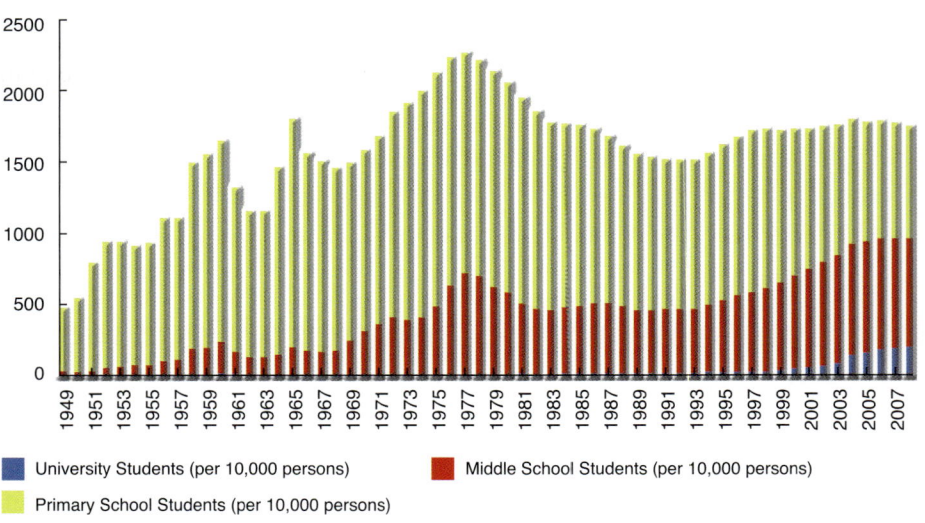

Source: *China Statistics Yearbook (1949–2007)* and *China Statistics Summary (2009)*, China National Bureau of Statistics.

China's educational system (1949–2008).

Secondly, men and women have received equal access to education. In schools at various levels, the proportion of female students was 43.7% in 1978 and increased to 47.1% in 2000. The proportion of female teachers was 32.5% in 1978 and increased to 46.3% in 2000. As China's educational system develops and improves, the overall quality of the population has been improving steadily with men and women both receiving equal access to education, thus accumulating human capital for sustainable development of the economy.

Medical and health care conditions have also improved on an annual basis, which has played an important role in improving the quality of life of the population. Since 1949, many serious infectious and parasitic diseases have been brought under control and have been eradicated. Indicators including the average life expectancy and infant and child mortality rates have improved significantly. China was hailed by the World Health Organization (WHO), World Bank, and other organizations as a model for developing countries and praised her efforts at using only 1% of the world's health resources to address the health care problems for 22% of the world's population. In recent years, as China's public expenditure on health care increased, health care resources have become more abundant and readily available. Both the number of practicing physicians and the number of beds in hospitals and health care institutions have increased. Medical performance of hospitals and health care institutions were improved through the process of market competition and integration. In 2008, there were 59,572 hospitals and health care institutions with more than 2.082 million practicing physicians and more than 4 million beds.

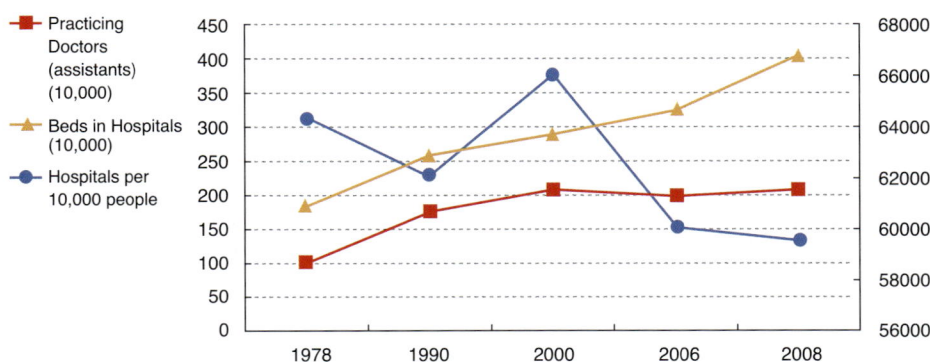

Source: *China Statistics Yearbook (1978–2008)* and *China Statistics Summary (2009)*, China National Bureau of Statistics.

China's heath care system (1978–2008).

A Higher Standard of Living

Since the reform and opening up, the per capita disposable income of urban residents has increased significantly. It rose from RMB 343 in 1978 to RMB 1,510 in 1990, and further increased to RMB 15,781 in 2008. The per capita net income of rural residents has also increased significantly, from RMB 134 in 1978 to RMB 686 in 1990 and peaking at RMB 4,761 in 2008. The per capita consumer expenditure has also risen substantially, reaching RMB 11,243 for urban residents and RMB 3,661 for rural residents in 2008. In addition, China's urban and rural residents' savings have increased substantially, from RMB 20.16 billion in 1978 to RMB 21.79 trillion in 2008, while outstanding savings per capita rose from RMB 22 in 1978 to RMB 16,407 in 2008.

In general, the Engel coefficient for China has been decreasing annually for both urban and rural residents. The Engel coefficient for urban households dropped from 57.5% in 1978 to 37.9% in 2008 while that of the rural households dropped from 67.7% in 1978 to 43.7% in 2008.

The housing conditions of residents have also continuously improved since the reform and opening up. From 1990 to 2008, urban dwelling space per capita increased from 14.7 square meters to 32.4 square meters, while rural dwelling space per capita increased from 17.8 square meters to 32.4 square meters. Urban dwelling space and housing quality will be further improved as

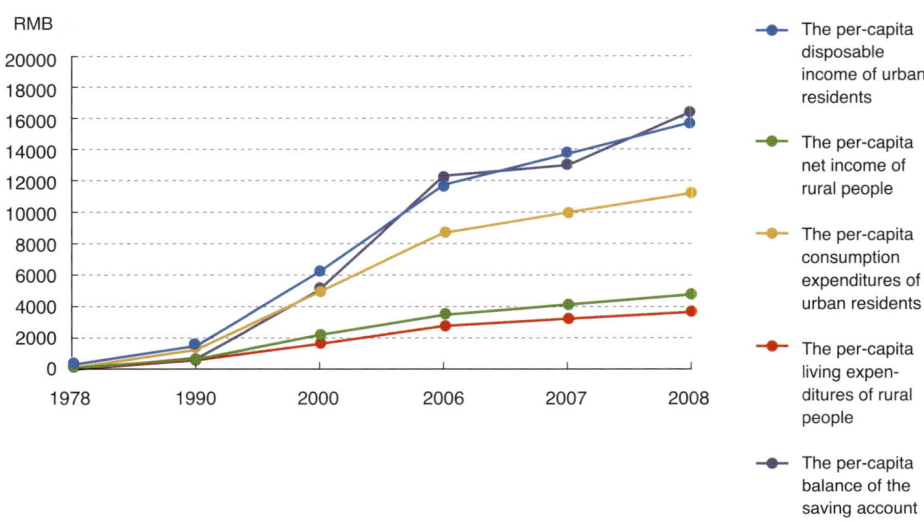

Source: *China Statistics Yearbook (2008), China Statistics Summary (2009)* and *Collection of the Statistical Data of New China during 50 Years,* China National Bureau of Statistics.

Living standards in China: incomes and expenditures (1978–2008).

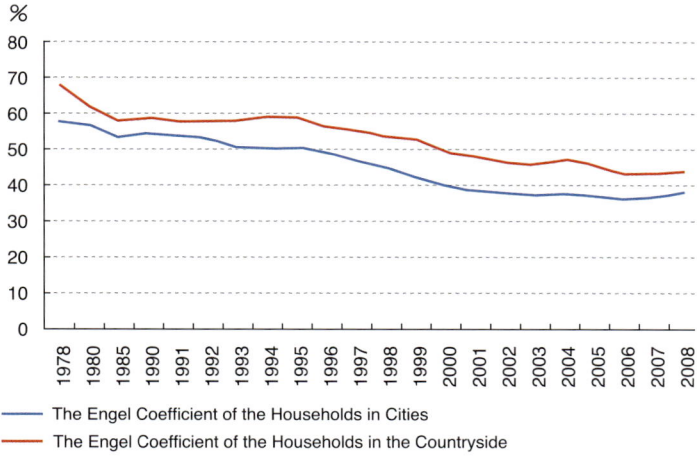

Source: *China Statistics Yearbook (2008)*, China National Bureau of Statistics.

Engel coefficients in the cities and the countryside of China (1978–2008).

China's large-scale construction of government-subsidized housing continues. The government's focus on rural construction will also create significant improvements in living conditions there.

Since China's founding, her level of urbanization has improved in parallel with the development of her economy and urban construction. The level of urbanization increased from 10% in 1949 to 45.7% in 2008. The process has further accelerated since reform and opening up began in 1978. Most recently, the construction of small towns and development of the countryside has led to a rapid increase in the level of urbanization.

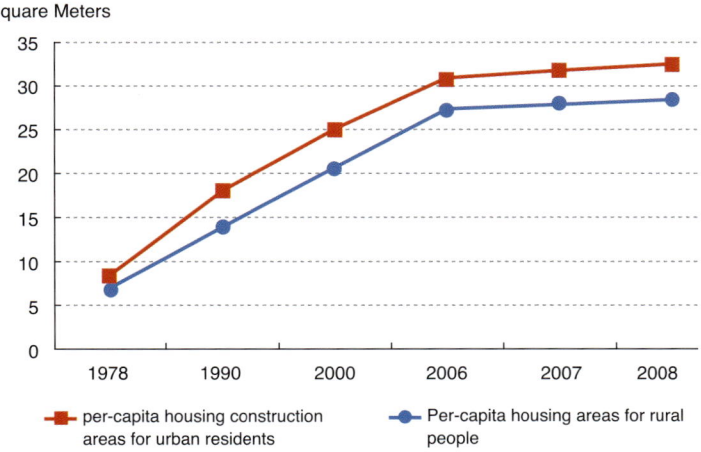

Source: *China Statistics Yearbook (2008)*, China Statistics Bureau.

Housing conditions in China (1978–2008).

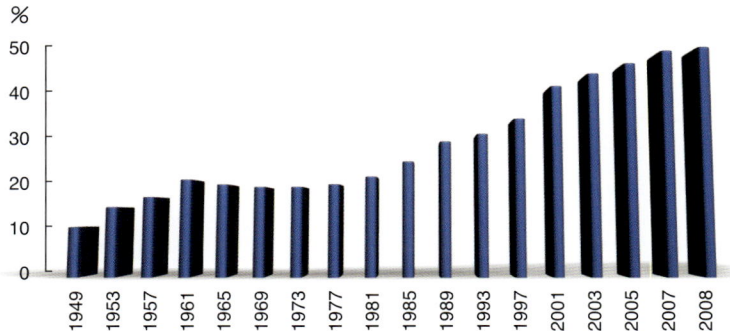

Urbanization in China (1949–2008).

The coverage of China's social security system has also increased in recent years. The number of people participating in old-age insurance, medical insurance, unemployment insurance, work-related injury insurance, and maternity insurance has grown considerably. Between 2007 and 2008, the number of migrant workers participating in urban medical insurance rose from 11.18 million to 42.49 million, while those participating in work-related injury insurance increased from 9.96 million to 49.76 million. The new rural cooperative health care program has reached 2,729 counties, with a participation rate of 91.5%. Great progress has been made in rural poverty alleviation as well. Using the 2008 rural poverty standard of per capita annual income of RMB 1,196, the number of those living below the poverty line (low-income and absolutely poverty-stricken population) in rural areas at the end of 2008 was 40.07 million, 3.13 million less than the 43.2 million calculated according to the 2007 rural poverty standard of RMB 1,067 in per capita annual income.

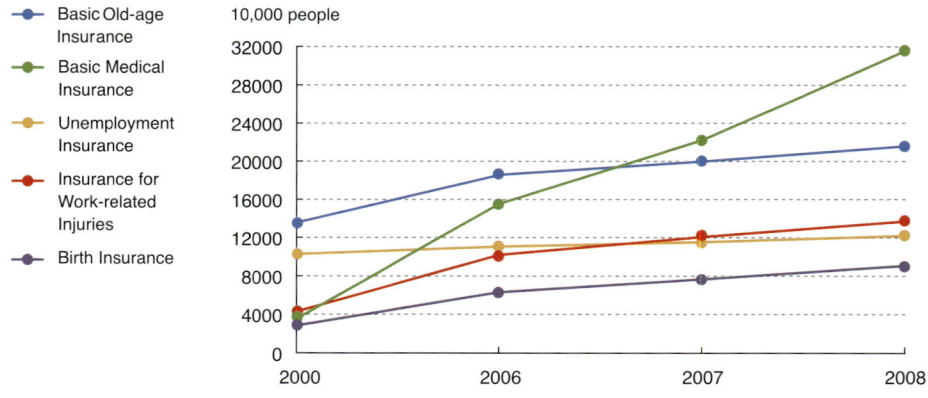

Source: *China Statistics Yearbook (2008)* and *Statistical Bulletin of National Social and Economic Development in 2008 of People's Republic of China,* China National Bureau of Statistics.

Social security in China (2000–2008).

Chapter 5

China's Challenges and Her Economic Development Trends

Incredible achievements have been made in the last 60 years of China's economic development. Since the strengthening of China's economy, the foundations and conditions of her economic development have also changed. Now, there exist both adverse factors that impede development as well as favorable factors that promote development. China's government is working to implement her scientific mode of development, which minimizes adverse factors and utilizes favorable factors by using timely and effective macro-control measures to advance economic growth, thereby leading China's economy forward to the benefit of the Chinese people.

Adverse Factors That Restrict China's Economic Development

The most critical factors restricting China's future economic development are energy and resource shortages. Although China enjoys a rich resource base, her large population results in relatively low levels of energy resources per capita. China's per capita share of coal and water resources is only 50% of the world's average, while her per capita share of oil and natural gas is only about one-fifteenth of the world's average. At the same time, China's low energy utilization rate of 32% is 10% lower than that of developed countries, which is a striking difference. China also lags behind developed countries in the development of new and renewable energy sources such as nuclear power, solar energy, wind energy, tidal energy, and geothermal energy. Coal accounts for as much as 76% of China's primary energy production and consumption— the highest rate in the world—compared to an average of only 21.4% for industrialized countries and a global average of 26.5%. In addition to exerting excessive pressure on the environment, the high level of coal usage results in an inefficient energy system.

China's domestic energy resources of oil and natural gas also have difficulties in meeting the needs of modernization. China became a net oil importer in 1993 and her oil imports have since increased from the then 9.88 million tons to more than 200 million tons in 2008, causing her dependence on foreign oil to rise from 6.4% of demand to a whopping 52%! China's increasing dependence on oil imports and her lack of strategic oil reserves makes her vulnerable to the impact of changes in global crude oil prices. In the coming years, oil shortages will be the biggest threat to China's energy security.

Urban social problems have started to rear their ugly heads in China. In 2009, China's output and sales volume of automobiles exceeded 13 million, giving China the distinction of being the world's largest producer and market for automobiles. This picture, taken in August 2009, shows traffic congestion in Beijing's central business district.

As energy demand rises, higher emissions of major pollutants exert more pressure on the environment. Environmental pollution and ecological deterioration have already reached critical levels in some areas. Air, water, and soil pollution have become increasingly serious while pollution caused by solid wastes, vehicle exhausts, and organic pollutants continue to rise.

Moreover, environmental pollution has also spread to rural areas. China's use of pesticides to control insect damages to crops have achieved remarkable results over the past 10 years. Although the coverage of pesticide use has expanded to 1.5 million square kilometers per year and the quantity of chemical fertilizers used has reached 29.3 million tons, the rate of effective application of chemical fertilization reach only 30%; only half the level achieved in advanced agricultural regions overseas. The rest either evaporated into the atmosphere or flowed into the soil, rivers, and lakes, turning water bodies eutrophic and producing excessive amounts of nitrate in sources of drinking water. The degradation of more than 90% of the natural grassland throughout the country has resulted in a significant loss in biodiversity. At the same time, economic development and population growth have been accompanied by a rapidly deteriorating global environment, including the depletion of the ozone layer, destruction of tropical rain forests, increased greenhouse gases, acid rain,

Economic growth has also brought along pollution. This picture, taken on August 19, 2009, shows a blue-green algae bloom in Wuhan's East Lake, Hubei Province.

and other environmental problems. These pose a serious threat to humanity's survival and continued development. Ecological destruction and environmental pollution are not only detrimental to people's lives and health, but have also caused tremendous losses to China's economy.

A second factor restricting China's economic development is her low level of urbanization. Despite improvements over many years of China's level of urbanization, where it reached 45.7% in 2008, the need for urbanization is still great and a large proportion of the rural population has yet to leave the countryside. According to current standards, a country is considered modern if at least 60% of her total population lives in cities. To meet this basic standard, China must relocate 200 million peasants to the cities. As these migrants enter the cities, the government must invest in cultural, educational, and public facilities to assist them to adapt to urban lifestyles. Simultaneously, industrialization and the creation of new jobs are required to support these 200 million migrants. The government faces the complex tasks of developing the economy, improving the methods of economic development, and enhancing the future potential and innovation of economic development, while creating new job

China faces the challenge of improving the skill levels of her abundant rural laborers. This will help to narrow the income gap between urban and rural workers. This picture, taken on February 25, 2009, shows laborers from Lianyungang, Jiangsu Province, enrolled in free government-sponsored sewing courses.

opportunities. At the same time, problems such as the limited amount of per capita arable land and resources challenge China's resources and environment in supporting urbanization and modernization.

China's reform and opening up have promoted the rapid economic and social development of urban and rural areas and her achievements have attracted worldwide attention. As the level of urbanization has rose, both the material and spiritual life of urban and rural residents has improved considerably. However, the fundamental characteristics of China's dual urban–rural structure remain unchanged. Urban and rural residents are still treated as if they belong to two different worlds. As seen from the difference in urban and rural residents' levels of per capita income and consumption, social security, medical and health care, and cultural education, there remains a wide gap between urban and rural areas. Despite the implementation of policies attempting to balance urban and rural development in recent years, the differences between urban and rural areas have not fundamentally changed.

A third factor restricting economic development is the serious imbalance in the level of economic development between different regions. Because of differences between regions in their economic foundations and natural conditions, China's economic development remains skewed toward the east and away from the west. Furthermore, this imbalance continues to deepen. Despite the successive implementation in recent years of the strategies of "Develop the Western Region," "Rejuvenate the Industrial Hub of the Northeast," and the "Emergence of Central China," the problem of imbalanced economic development between regions remains unsolved, presenting a challenge to China's future economic development.

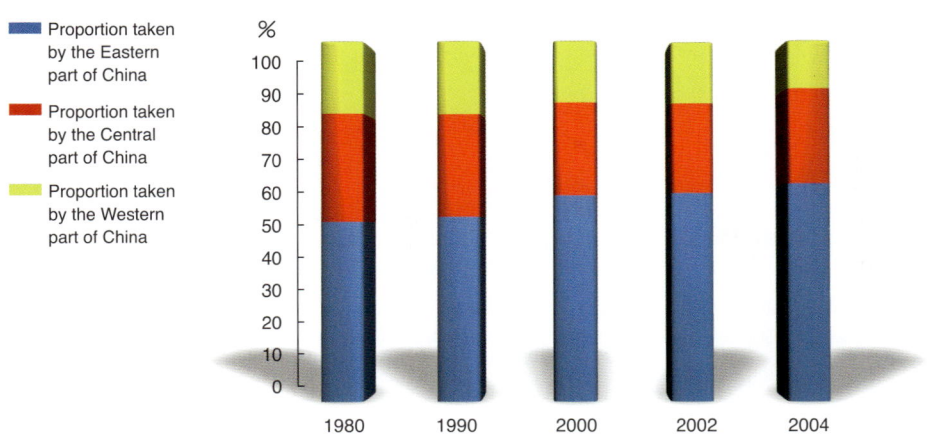

Regional economic imbalances in China (1980–2004).

Fourthly, the wide income gap is not conducive to maintain a sustained and stable economic growth in future. China is a large country, and while future development cannot be achieved without full utilization of foreign resources and markets, fundamentally speaking, there is a need to rely on the domestic market to support continued economic development through expanding domestic demand. The effective expansion of domestic demand cannot be achieved without first narrowing the income gap. The income distribution gap between urban and rural residents has been growing along with China's economic development. The proportion of disposable income of the Chinese accounted for by urban-residents has been rising, while the proportion accounted for by rural residents has been declining. Although China's rural–urban gap was narrowed to some extent during the Sixth Five-Year Plan (1980–1985) due to a rapid increase in farmers' income, the gap has since widened continuously between the subsequent Seventh Five-Year Plan (1986–1990) and Ninth Five-Year Plan (1996 to 2000).

In terms of income distribution, considerable differences exist among varying groups and classes, as seen in the proportional decrease of income for low- and middle- income groups with a proportional increase of income for high-income groups, leading to a trend of higher income being earned by the high-income group. Based on the World Bank's *World Development Report 2006,* the Gini coefficient[1] of China dropped from 0.16 in 1978 to 0.47 in 2006,

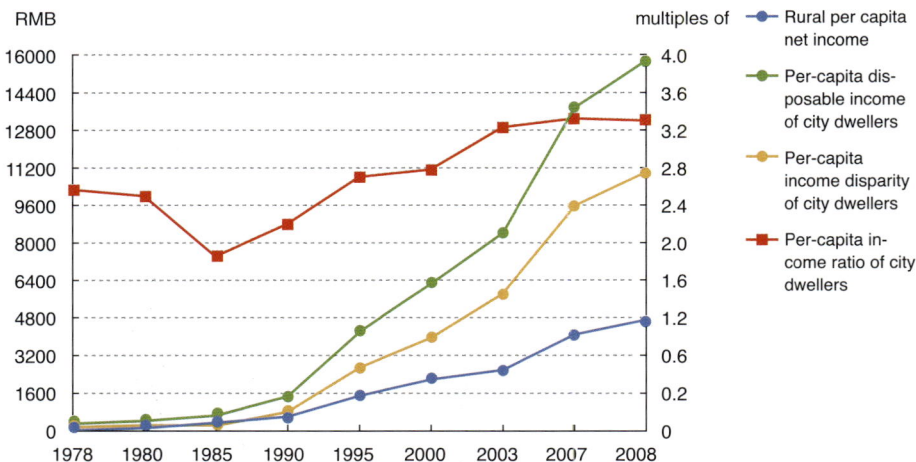

Source: *China Statistics Yearbook 2008* and *Statistical Bulletin of National Social and Economic Development in 2008 of People's Republic of China,* China National Bureau of Statistics.

Imbalanced income distributions between the urban and rural areas (1978–2008).

---

[1]The Gini coefficient measures the gap between the rich and the poor, with 0 being perfect equality and 1 being perfect inequality.

exceeding both the international alert level and the level used by the rest of the world's developed nations. The imbalance in income distribution will have several adverse effects on economic and social development. Firstly, the slow rise in farmers' income and the growth of urban low-income groups will seriously hamper the development of urban and rural markets and the expansion of consumer demand. Secondly, a widening income gap as a result of monopolies and unfair competition reduces both efficiency and people's initiative for production and creativity. Thirdly, resentment toward corruption and unfair income distribution affects social stability.

The fifth factor inhibiting sustained and stable future economic development is corruption and the inefficiencies arising from an imperfect economic and political system. From the institutional standpoint of China's economic development, whilst she is undergoing a massive economic and social transformation, the newly established market economy system is still imperfect and the transformation of the government's economic role is not yet complete. These elements are not conducive to maintain a sustained and stable economic development. At the fundamental level, the democratic system is the most basic guarantee of socialist equity and efficiency also needs to be improved. Without the guarantee of a perfect socialist democratic system, the Chinese government cannot eradicate corruption among her officials and the distortions in economic activities, thus posing a problem to achieving "common prosperity" for all Chinese people.

Factors for Promoting Economic Development

China is a large developing country with a long history and a splendid civilization. She may have fallen relatively behind other countries in terms of industrialization, but for the last 60 years, she has shown the ability and confidence to stand on her own two feet and catch up with the world's other developed countries. Though China is confronted with many adverse conditions and challenges in her path to economic success, she possesses many favorable conditions and advantages.

Firstly, China operates a socialist market economy system. In this system, public ownership is dominant while coexisting with and developing alongside other diverse forms of ownership. Distribution is done according to work completed while supplemented by other methods, and primary distribution emphasizes efficiency while secondary distribution emphasizes equity. China's unique ownership structure and distribution system have assured rapid growth of her economy throughout the past 30 years and will also be advantageous for the sustainable development of her economy in the future. China is able to achieve a balance between reform, development, and stability by promoting development through reform and maintaining stability through development. The management of important and natural monopoly industries by the government on behalf of her people is assured by the dominance of public ownership, while the development of other diverse forms of ownership encourages foreign investors and domestic entrepreneurs to utilize their own initiative in economic pursuits. The distribution system reflects the pursuit of socialism with her Chinese characteristics: allow some people to get rich first and then with their support, help the remaining people to achieve common prosperity.

Secondly, the Chinese people have a strong desire to build a prosperous, democratic, civilized, and harmonious country. Over a period of 5,000 years of development, China has developed a strong, industrious, brave, and peace-loving national spirit of solidarity and unity with patriotism at its core; a spiritual legacy that has sustained the Chinese nation for generations. Since the reform and opening up, the Chinese people have used socialist modernization to build a socialist core value system. While conducive to China's economic development, the national spirit and socialist core value system have become a powerful spiritual force promoting the development and progress of contemporary China.

Thirdly, China's ruling party and government's capabilities for macroeconomic policy have been improving. In the past 60 years, it has been proven that the Communist Party of China and the government under her leadership are capable of coordinating and handling various complex relationships and problems to steadily develop China's economy. Throughout the process of reform and development, the government's macroeconomic policymaking has also improved. In order to see how China's macroeconomic policy measures have evolved, the "soft landing" that occurred from 1993 to 1996 can be used as a turning point. From 1978 to 1991, the Chinese government's policy measures were mainly administrative and focused on planning while the objective was mainly to control inflation. After 1992, the market economy system was introduced. Since then, the government's macroeconomic management techniques have shifted from administrative and planning measures to legal measures, and were often supplemented by direct administrative measures and government investments. Fiscal and monetary policies play an increasingly important role as such measures aim to control inflation and prevent deflation, because oversupply of goods will become increasingly common since the era of food and product shortages transits to an economy marked by the twin possibilities of inflation and deflation. The Chinese government has demonstrated solid performances in the six rounds of macroeconomic policymaking since reform and opening up began.

The success of the government's macroeconomic policy measures was further demonstrated in 2008. At the beginning of the year when price

China's national spirit is the strong driving force of her development. This picture, taken on May 14, 2008, shows a long line of blood donors in Nanjing, awaiting their turns to help the Sichuan earthquake victims.

inflation accelerated and heated up the economy, the government deployed macroeconomic policy and administrative measures along the line of "double prevention."[2] As the world's financial markets became more tumultuous, China's rate of export growth decreased sharply while inflationary pressure fell and downward pressure on the economy began to appear. As a result, the government shifted her macroeconomic policy from "double prevention" to "maintain and control"[3] and declared that the primary goal was to maintain stable and rapid economic development, and curb the rapid rise in prices.

In the fourth quarter, the impact of the international financial crisis on the real economy became evident; world economic growth slowed sharply and the negative impact on China's economic development became increasingly clear. The government then shifted her macroeconomic policy to an "active fiscal policy and moderately loose monetary policy" and focused on promoting growth, expanding domestic demand, adjusting the economy's structure, and improving people's livelihoods, in order to solve immediate problems and increase future development potential. The government simultaneously introduced a package of fiscal, monetary, and industrial policies and measures that played an important role in alleviating the impact of severe natural disasters (such as

---

[2]Prevent over-investments and price inflation.

[3]Maintain steady economic growth and control price inflation.

heavy snow and blizzards in the south, the Sichuan earthquake, and so on) and the global financial crisis on China's economy, while maintaining sound and rapid economic development. The improvement of the government's macro-economic policymaking helped China's economy maintain a steady and healthy development.

Fourthly, China's abundant labor can assure long-term rapid economic growth. The labor force is one of the critical elements used for promoting economic growth, affecting both the structure of a country's industry and resources. Although the conflict between a massive labor force and limited resources is evident, a large population does not necessarily push China's development into a Malthusian trap. On the contrary, China can achieve economic growth by using her abundant labor as a competitive advantage in international trade. Since the reform and opening up, China has relied on her ample labor force to pursue competitive advantages in labor-intensive industries, and achieved sustained economic growth by utilizing the strategy of competitive advantage. Although China is currently changing her economic growth model, labor-intensive industries are still needed to ensure a sufficient level of employment and further the transfer of rural labor to cities and towns. Alongside advances in agricultural production technology, more surplus rural labor needs

China possesses a competitive advantage in international trade due to her abundant labor resources and increasing numbers of high-skilled workers. This picture, taken on July 11, 2009, shows a job fair for graduates in Huai'an, Jiangsu Province.

to be shifted to urban areas. This low-skilled labor force can ensure that China maintains her competitive advantage in labor resources in international trade.

An increased level of education and improved health conditions will further develop China's human resources, thereby improving the accumulation of human capital, which is a critical element for economic growth. As shown by the world's history of economic development, the contribution of human capital to economic growth has been increasing. An empirical study of China's economy demonstrates that human capital is playing an increasingly important role in China's economic growth.

The fifth advantageous factor for China's economic development is a relatively relaxed international environment, which has improved tremendously for China since the 1950s to 1960s. In the early 1970s, China returned to the UN and successively established diplomatic relations with the United States, Japan, and many other developed countries. After the reform and opening up, China opened her doors to the outside world and the world beckoned China. In the 1990s, China formally proposed the establishment of a socialist market economy system, which further eliminated several barriers between China's

FYI
FOR YOUR INFORMATION

THE MALTHUSIAN TRAP

Demographic evidence shows that early populations experienced high birth rates and high mortality rates, with an overall trend of slow population growth as the latter offsets the former. After the industrial revolution, the "two highs and one low," (high birth rate, high mortality rate, low growth rate) population growth model in Western nations was replaced by the "three lows" model (low birth rate, low mortality rate, low growth rate) within one hundred years.

Thomas Malthus believed that war, famine, and pestilence were all means to stabilize population growth to a level compatible with food supply, based on the implicit logic that population size had to be in proportion to agricultural development. Malthus believed that population size had to be intermittently reduced in some ways, as he saw that population growth advanced in accordance with a geometric series, whereas food supply only increased in accordance with an arithmetic series. The "Malthusian Trap" thus described the inability of a population to advance beyond the corresponding level of agricultural development.

economy and the international economy. Within a relaxed international environment, China can better concentrate on building the economy and utilize foreign resources and markets for her own development. China's accession to the WTO in 2001 expanded China's platform for using the international market and further integrated China into the tide of economic globalization. In recent years, China's dependence on foreign trade has increased, her total import and export volume has risen and her overseas investments have spread far and wide. All these developments indicate that China is integrating deeper into the global economy. China can fully utilize domestic and international resources to achieve an optimal allocation of resources and provide more opportunities for adjusting her industrial structure and boosting economic competitiveness.

Development of China's Future Economy with the "Three-Step" Strategy[4]

As early as the 1950s to 1960s, the Chinese government put forward the ambitious goal of achieving the "four modernizations"[5] by the end of the twentieth century. After the reform and opening up began in 1978, Deng Xiaoping put forward a "three step" strategy for China's economic development in accordance with China's basic national conditions and possibilities for economic development. The strategy was later improved upon. The goals of the strategy are:

- to quadruple the gross national economy by the end of the twentieth century in order to achieve a higher level of well-being;
- establish a perfect socialist market economy system by 2021 and achieve a high standard of well-being; and
- achieve a level of modernization equal to other medium-developed countries by 2049, the 100th anniversary of the founding of the People's Republic of China.

Between 1953 and 2005, China implemented 10 Five-Year Plans. China began to implement the 11th Five-Year Plan in 2006, a crucial period that

---

[4]The "first step": double the GDP in 1990 as compared to 1981, hence solving the pressing issues of food shortage and adequate housing. The "second step": double the GDP by 2000 as compared to 1991, hence achieving better quality of lives for the Chinese people. The "third step": by 2049, the Chinese people will be well-off and live in a modernized society, with the average per capita GDP at the level of a medium-developed country.
[5]This refers to the modernization of industry, agriculture, science and technology, and national defense.

AIMS OF THE 11TH FIVE-YEAR PLAN (2006–2010)

During the 11th Five-Year Plan period (2006–2010), China needs to achieve sustained, rapid, coordinated, and healthy development of her economy and society, while making measured progress in the ongoing stage of building a relatively prosperous society. China needs to double her annual per capita GDP by 2010 as compared to 2000, while improving efficiency and reducing consumption. The plan asks for

- significant improvements in resource utilization;
- reducing energy consumption per unit GDP by about 20% as compared to the end of the 10th Five-Year period;
- halting the trend of ecological and environmental deterioration and effectively curbing excessive loss of arable land;
- fostering a group of superior enterprises with independent intellectual property rights, well-known brands, and strong international competitiveness;
- making the socialist market economy system relatively perfect as the economy reaches new levels of openness while maintaining a balance of international payments;
- popularizing and consolidating the nine-year compulsory education program;
- increasing work opportunities in urban areas;
- significantly reducing the number of people living in poverty and ensuring the soundness of the social security system;
- improving the income levels and the quality of life of urban and rural residents, stabilizing the overall price levels and improving conditions in housing, transportation, education, culture, health care, and the environment;
- progressing toward building democracy and the legal system and developing socialist culture and ethics;
- improving social security and workplace safety; and
- making new progress in building a harmonious society.

relied on past achievements while paving the way for future efforts to build a relatively prosperous society. The development goals set for the 11th Five-Year Plan are:

- to continue the outstanding development momentum of the previous stage while laying a solid foundation for development in the next decade;
- to stay focused on the goal of building a relatively prosperous society while reflecting on the phased development nature of the five-year period;

China has imbued a new meaning in the term of "moderately prosperous society" for the twenty-first century.

E-commerce is playing an increasingly important role in China's modern economy.

- to demonstrate a positive attitude and give hope to and inspire the people to create positive market expectations, while at the same time, formulate realistic and feasible measures in consideration of developmental bottleneck constraints, and adequately evaluate various uncertain issues to ensure achievement of the development goal from 2006 to 2010.

In 2007, the 17th CPC National People's Congress promulgated a new requirement for building a relatively prosperous society: quadruple the per capita GDP of 2000 by the year 2020. This marked a modification of the original goal from quadrupling overall GDP to quadrupling per capita GDP. The goal of building a relatively prosperous society is not merely an economic development indicator, but rather a goal consistent with accelerating the modernization process, and it is closely linked with the goal of developing socialism with Chinese characteristics. For this reason, the central government further expanded the goal of "building a prosperous, strong, democratic, and civilized modern socialist country" to "building a prosperous, strong, democratic, civilized, and harmonious modern socialist country." In order to meet this new requirement, China needs to:

- enhance developmental coordination to achieve rapid and sound economic development;

- expand socialist democracy to better protect people's rights and social equity and justice;
- strengthen cultural development to improve the nation's cultural and ethical qualities;
- accelerate the development of social efforts to improve the people's lives;
- build an environmentally sustainable civilization and industrial structure, growth model and consumption pattern that are beneficial for preserving energy resources and protecting the environment.

After achieving the goal of building a relatively prosperous society around 2021, China, the largest developing country with a long history and an ancient civilization, would have basically accomplished her industrialization drive, and her overall national strength would have been significantly increased while the domestic market would be the largest in the world. China would have seen a general increase in the people's affluence and standard of living, as well as possess a healthy and clean environment. Furthermore, the Chinese people will enjoy full democratic rights and have greater cultural and ethical values as well as more developed spiritual pursuits. China's structural systems would have improved and her society will be more vibrant, stable, and united. China will also become more open to the outside world and make greater contributions to humanity.

Chapter 6

China's Role and Position in the Global Economy

Alongside China's economic development, worldwide opinions regarding China have increased in recent years. Some expressed optimisms about China's future and believed that China is bound to rise; others are pessimistic and believed that China's economy is about to collapse. Some suggested that China is a threat to the world regardless of whether she rises or collapses and they predict that China's development and transformation will go against world peace and prosperity. In fact, China's development has become an important factor in promoting world harmony, and the application of the "harmonious world" theory will lead to more active efforts to smoothen the relationship between China and the world. China will continue to be the engine of world economic development while acting as a stabilizing force for world peace, and also catalyze further advancement of world civilizations.

China: An Important Member of the Global Economic Community

China's dream of becoming an important and indispensable member of the global community began when Sun Yat-sen overthrew the imperial monarchy and established the Republic of China in 1912. The founding of the People's Republic of China in 1949 achieved national independence for China and earned the necessary respect from people around the world. But due to the Cold War, China has very little diplomatic relations with the Western capitalist nations led by the United States. In the 1970s, as international relations warmed, China resumed her legitimate seat in the UN, and successively established diplomatic relations with major Western countries.

After resuming her legitimate seat at the UN in 1971, China was qualified to join the General Agreement on Tariffs and Trade (GATT) but was unable to do so due to the international political structure in which, according to socialist theory, the world market was divided into two camps. For this reason, China saw foreign trade only as a means of supplementing production and limited its functions to the regulation of supply and demand as well as trading of essential products. As a result, China did not take full advantage of the international division of labor and exchange and did not attach any significance to utilizing her competitive advantages through making full use of foreign resources and markets. Between 1953 and 1978, China's share of the world exports declined from 1.23% to 0.75%, sliding down from 17th to 32nd in the world rankings.

After the reform and opening up in 1978, the Chinese government sized up the situation and decided that peace and development were the dominant trends of the world, and that war could be avoided completely. China could take advantage of the trend for global economic development to actively introduce and make use of advanced foreign technologies and attract investment from overseas to develop her own economy. In the meantime, China could also join the global community and trade with other countries. In September 1982, China applied for "observer" status in GATT and petitioned for the resumption of her status as a GATT contracting party in July 1986.

In 2001, after 15 years of negotiations of rejoining GATT and entering the WTO, China finally achieved her goals of becoming a member of the global economic community. Joining the WTO was an inevitable choice, considering China's wish to make use of the international division of labor and utilize the trend of economic globalization. China's accession to the WTO also initiated a process of increased global economic activity that would bring benefits to every country, including China herself. The accession to the WTO would enable China to carry out international trade and economic cooperation under the multilateral, stable, and unconditional most-favored-nation treatment granted by WTO members. China will also further open up her domestic markets such as goods and services, while at the same time actively implement the "going abroad" strategy to promote a wider and deeper participation in international economic affairs, thus creating a more favorable international environment for

China's modernization drive. China's accession to the WTO would enhance the impact of the international market operating mechanisms on China's domestic market, helping China to improve her own market mechanisms and cultivate her market system to allocate social resources more effectively, and thus achieve a reasonable flow of goods and production factors. Relying on these organizational institutions, China can actively tap on domestic and foreign resources and markets to develop her own economy, so as to add more vibrancy to the world economy.

Being an active participant in economic globalization, China also plays a key role in regional economic organizations and development. Economic globalization and regionalization are two major trends in the development of the global economy; any country seeking economic development would not ignore them. Being a large developing country, China will conform to the historical trend of continuously integrating herself into the world's economic development. China will not develop if she is isolated from the rest of the world, whereas the world will not develop without China's participation. As China is firmly committed to opening up, she will never again pursue any isolationist policy.

China's official entry into the WTO in November 2001 signifies that she has become an important part of the global economy.

At the 60th anniversary of the UN on September 15, 2005, President Hu Jintao made an important speech entitled "Strive to Build a Harmonious World of Lasting Peace and Common Prosperity." He pointed out that China's economic development benefited from global peace and stability and would not pose any threat to the international community. Furthermore, China would diligently link her own development with that of humanity by making the most of world peace, while using her development to maintain world peace and promote common prosperity. China's development would not stand in the way of any country that pose a threat, but instead contribute to world peace, stability, and common prosperity.

In the midst of a worsening global financial crisis since 2008, China has made her intentions clear by sending a message of confidence and cooperation to the rest of the world. At the London Summit of the G-20[1] in April 2009,

The first round of the Sino-US Strategic and Economic Dialogues was held in Washington D.C., on July 27, 2009. President Obama met with the visiting Chinese State Councilor Dai Bingguo and Vice Premier Wang Qishan. Wang expressed that a more open and energetic Chinese economy will bring about opportunities not only to the United States but also to other countries.

---

[1]Group of Twenty Finance Ministers and Central Bank Governors.

President Hu Jintao put forward a four-point proposal for promoting global economic growth, reiterating that China would make her due contribution to global economic growth by actively participating in international efforts to cope with the global financial crisis. On behalf of the Chinese government, President Hu Jintao declared that "as all nations of the world are in the same boat facing the violent winds and fierce waves of the global financial crisis, everybody onboard needs to work together to overcome the current difficulties so that this boat can sail through the financial turmoil safe and sound. Then, the negative effects of the financial crisis can be reduced to a minimum and an early recovery of the global economy would be possible."

At the Finance Ministers' and Central Bank Governors' meeting of the G-20 held during September 4–5, 2009, China's Finance Minister Xie Xuren said that the plan by the Chinese government to promote economic growth had yield significant results and therefore the economy had begun to stabilize and recover, although the foundation was not concrete and firm. Hence, the government would continue to implement a proactive fiscal policy and moderately loose monetary policy to consolidate and stabilize the recovery, and achieve a steady and rapid development of the economy. He also pointed out that the current world economy was at a critical period of recovery and all countries should maintain the continuity and stability of macroeconomic policies and oppose all forms of protectionism so as to promote global economic recovery. He stressed that all countries should work together to promote reform of international financial institutions and adjust the shares and voting rights structures to significantly increase representation and voice of the developing countries.

Zhou Xiaochuan, Governor of the People's Bank of China, said at the same meeting that all countries should continue to maintain close cooperation to promote economic recovery and stable operation of the financial system. He urged international financial organizations to strengthen early warning systems for crises; improve regulation; reduce the impact of cyclical elements in the financial system; enhance cross-border regulatory cooperation and crisis management; improve the objectivity, consistency, and effectiveness of international financial regulatory standards based on sovereignty in regulation; and improve and popularize core principles for effective deposit insurance systems and investor protection mechanisms.

China in the Globalized Economy

China's total volume of foreign trade in goods has increased substantially since the reform and opening up. Between 1978 and 2007, China's annual total volume of foreign trade in goods increased from RMB 35.5 billion to over RMB

16.67 trillion. During the same period, the total export volume of goods rose from RMB 16.76 billion to RMB 9.35 trillion, while the total import volume jumped from RMB 18.74 billion to RMB 7.33 trillion. Meanwhile, a trade deficit of RMB 19.8 billion turned into a trade surplus of RMB 2.02 trillion. At the same time, China's world ranking in terms of trade volume leaped from 29th to third place. China's rate of trade growth has changed along with the international business environment. For example, during the 1997 Asian financial crisis, China's trade volume grew at a relatively low rate. In 2008, China's trade volume increased only 17.8% over the previous year to US$2.56 trillion. Exports increased by 17.2% to US$1.43 trillion, while imports rose by 18.5% to US$1.13 trillion. China had a trade surplus of US$295.5 billion, an increase of US$32.8 billion over the previous year.

Another sign of China's transformation to a trading power is her increasing dependence on foreign trade; defined by the ratio between the total volume of foreign trade to GDP; and her trades' position in national economic activity. Due to international obstruction and the implementation of an import substitution strategy during the era of the planned economy, China's trade volume was relatively small. China mostly exported staple agricultural and secondary products in return for industrial equipments from other countries in the socialist bloc. After the reform and opening up, China's trade volume began to increase. China's dependence on foreign trade was quite low at first, registering less than

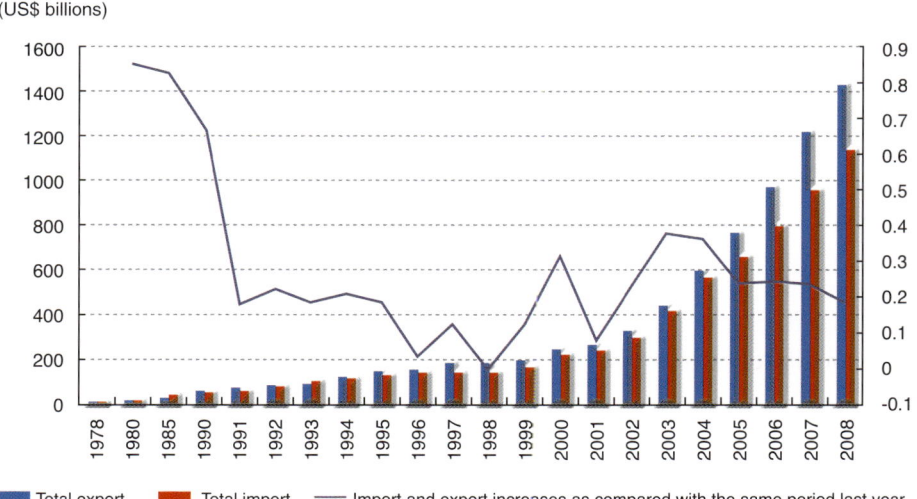

(US$ billions)

Total export   Total import   —— Import and export increases as compared with the same period last year

Source: *China Statistics Yearbook (2008)*, *China Statistics Summary (2008)*, and *Statistical Bulletin of National Social and Economic Development in 2008 of PRC*, China National Bureau of Statistics.

China's total imports and exports and their rates of increase (1978–2008).

10% in 1978. Since then, it has followed a generally upward trajectory, exceeding 30% in the 1990s. In recent years, it has reached about 65%. China's dependence on foreign trade is higher than the global average, indicating that large countries can also successfully implement an export-oriented development strategy.

The method, ratio, and structure of China's trade have changed significantly since 1978. Starting from the 1980s, China has been actively encouraging the inflow of foreign direct investments for setting up trading and processing enterprises that produce goods for export. These foreign-invested enterprises use their own foreign exchange funds to purchase imported raw materials and capital goods, then use foreign exchange funds to buy local currency for paying local staff and the expenses of local purchases. Their profits come from selling goods abroad. Under this policy, the processing trade sector of China's foreign trade has grown rapidly and consistently. In 1981, China's total volume of foreign trade was US$44 billion, of which the total volume of processing trade consisted of only US$2.6 billion. Processing trade exports have exceeded imports for every year since 1989, with the total volume of processing trade surpassing that of general trade every year since 1993. In 2008, the import and export volume of China's processing trade was US$1.05 trillion, accounting for 41% of the total. Processing trade exports reached US$675.18 billion, or 47.3%

Source: *China Statistics Yearbook (2008), China Statistics Summary (2008),* and *Statistical Bulletin of National Social and Economic Development in 2008 of People's Republic of China,* China National Bureau of Statistics.

China's reliance on foreign trade (1978–2008).

of total exports, while processing trade's surplus reached US$296.8 billion, making it the main source of China's overall trade surplus. The growing trade surplus was primarily due to the increase in foreign direct investments.

China's import/export structure has changed since 1978 with the proportion of manufactured goods decreasing, particularly in recent years. In 2008, the import volume of manufactured goods was US$770.31 billion, accounting for 68% of total imports, while the import volume of primary products accounted for 32%. The proportion of total exported volume of manufactured goods has increased significantly. In 2008, the export volume of manufactured goods was US$1.35 trillion, accounting for 95% of total exports, which marked a significant improvement to the 50% rate in 1985. The export of manufactured goods has become the main source of China's trade surplus. The substantial increase in the proportion accounted for by the export of manufactured goods is linked to the development of foreign-invested enterprises.

China's proportion of total world exports has been on the rise. In 1953, China's exports accounted for only 1.2% of the world total, but that figure had changed to 5.9% by 2003. By 2007, it had leapt to 8.9%, making China the world's second largest exporter after Germany. On July 22, 2009, the WTO announced that China would overtake Germany to become the world's largest exporter of goods. According to data published by the WTO in late August 2009, in the first half of the year, China surpassed Germany in terms of total exports and became the world's largest exporter.

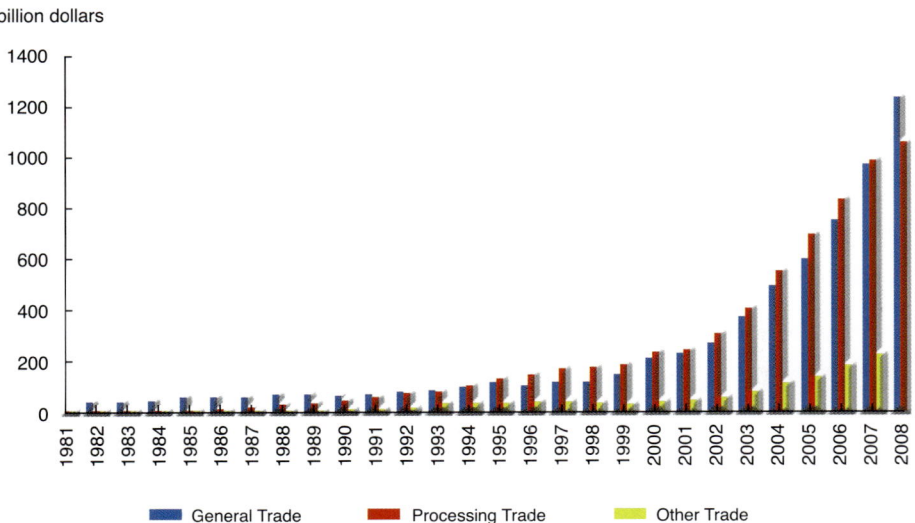

Source: *China Statistics Summary (2009),* China National Bureau of Statistics.

China's modes of trade (1981–2008).

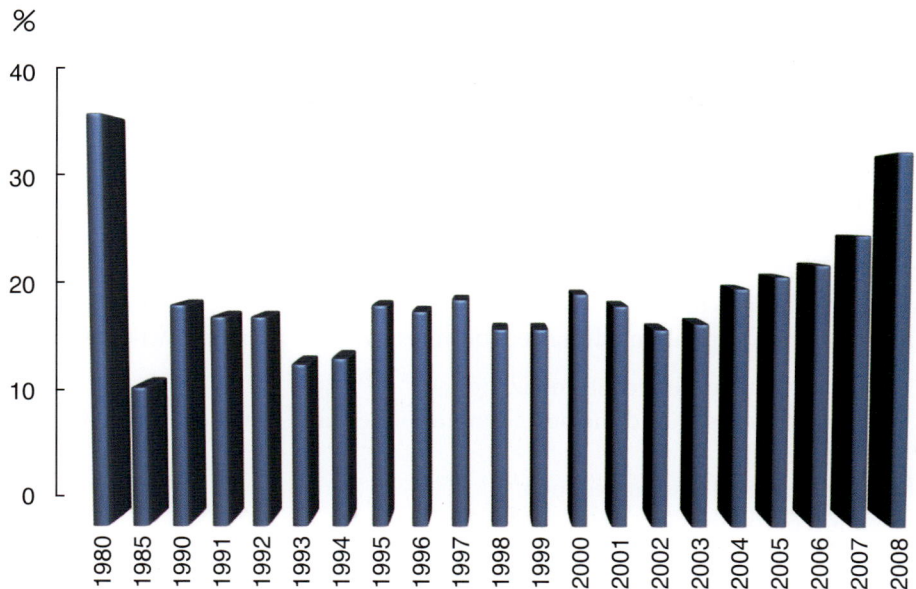

Source: *China Statistics Yearbook (2008)* and *China Statistics Summary (2009)*, China National Bureau of Statistics.

Proportion of imported primary products in China (1980–2008).

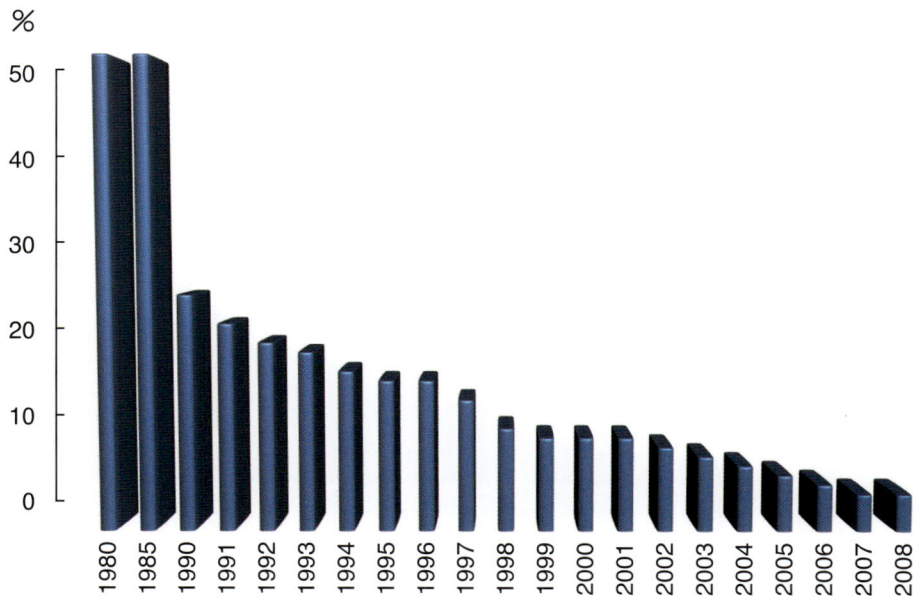

Source: *China Statistics Yearbook (2008)*, China National Bureau of Statistics.

Proportion of exported primary products in China (1980–2008).

In 2007, China's imports reached 6.8% of the global total, making her the world's third largest importer after the United States and Germany, at 14.5% and 7.6%, respectively.

The expansion of China's trade is related to the large-scale introduction of foreign capital. Since the reform and opening up, the amount of foreign capital in actual use in China, including foreign loans, foreign direct investments, and other foreign investments, has gradually increased. Foreign capital has been entering China rapidly since 1992. Foreign investments have made a relatively large contribution to China's economic development during this period. The effect of foreign capital on China's economy is evident in the following areas:

- marketization and internationalization;
- technology transfer and the development of new and advanced technologies;
- export growth;
- increase in fixed asset investments;
- creation of job opportunities; and
- improvement in the technology and management of China's SOEs and township enterprises through joint ventures, cooperation, and other methods.

The pace of foreign capital coming into China slowed down since the mid- to late-1990s, as seen in the continuous decrease in the proportion of China's GDP. However, the total amount is still increasing. At present, China ranks first in the world at attracting foreign investments. In 2008, China utilized US$92.4

Source: *China Statistics Summary (2009)*, China National Bureau of Statistics.

Foreign investments and the proportion of FDI in GDP (1979–2008).

billion of foreign direct investments, an increase of 23.6%, as compared with the same period of the previous year. The manufacturing sector accounted for 54% of the total, with the real estate sector taking up 20.1%.

China's economic cooperation with foreign countries has also increased significantly in recent years. Foreign projects accounted for US$56.6 billion in business in 2008, a 39.4% increase over 2007. Business from foreign labor service contracts reached US$8.1 billion, an increase of 19.1%.

Developing the Global Economy: China's Major Contributions

Since the founding of the People's Republic of China 60 years ago, she has gone through both planned and market economies. During the period of the planned economy, China established an independent national economic system and industrial hub, successfully developed nuclear weapons and satellite technology, and thus achieved her goal of becoming a world power. Operating as a market economy, China took advantage of the favorable situation and began to implement her reform and opening-up programs, bringing about rapid expansion of the economy and a substantial increase in per capita gross national income. Furthermore, China's volume of trade grew significantly and her major industrial and agricultural projects made it to the world's top ranking. Through her transformation, China is changing the world and gaining worldwide attention.

China's economy has performed strongly in recent years, maintaining a steady growth rate of 10%. This growth rate is higher than both the world average and that of developed economies. Among the BRIC countries (Brazil, Russia, India, and China), China's performance is the best. Among the 133 economies evaluated in the *2009-2010 Global Competitiveness Report* by the World Economic Forum, mainland China rose one place up to the 30th position and continues to lead amongst the BRIC countries.

China's economy in 2008 accounted for 7.23% of the overall world economy, putting it in third place behind the United States (23.44%) and Japan (8.09%). China's economic growth rate reached 9.0%, much higher than the global average growth rate of 3.4% and significantly higher than the average for the world's major countries and regions. Although the global financial crisis has cause serious impacts on countries around the world, China's economy alone has maintained her rapid rate of growth. In 2008, China's contribution to global economic growth exceeded 20%. While China's economy cannot develop in isolation from the rest of the world, neither can the global economy develop without China.

China's world rankings of major economic indicators

	1978	1990	2000	2005	2006	2007
GDP	10	11	6	4	4	4
Import/Export	27	16	8	3	3	3
Forex	38	7	2	2	1	1
Major Indutrial Output						
Steel	5	4	1	1	1	1
Coal	3	1	1	1	1	1
Crude Oil	8	5	5	5	6	5
Electricity	7	4	2	2	2	2
Cement	4	1	1	1	1	1
Chemical Fertilizer	3	3	1	1	1	1
Cotton Textiles	1	1	2	1	1	1
Major Agricultural Output						
Cereals	2	1	1	1	1	1
Meat	3	1	1	1	1	1
Cotton	2	1	1	1	1	1
Soybeans	3	3	4	4	4	4
Peanuts	2	2	1	1	1	1
Rape Seeds	2	1	1	1	1	1
Sugar Cane	7	4	3	3	3	2
Tea	2	2	2	1	1	1
Fruits	9	4	1	1	1	1

Source: *China Statistics Summary (2009)*, China National Bureau of Statistics.

Since the reform and opening up, China has made remarkable progress in developing her economy and promoting economic diversification while her achievements in improving the people's living standards have attracted world-wide attention. China's economy has achieved sustained and rapid growth over the past 30 over years, allowing her to play an increasingly important role in the global economy and be considered as one of the engines of world economic growth. She has a fast-growing market capacity and potential for further development. China's large volume of imports have helped her trading partners around the world and allowed some countries to escape from economic

Attractive and inexpensive China-made products have delivered material benefits to global consumers. This picture shows foreign buyers at a Haier Electrical booth of a trade fair held in China.

stagnation. China's attractive investment environment provides investors from various countries with business opportunities, making her the top choice for foreign investments. China's exported goods are both affordable and of high quality, meeting the needs of consumers in importing countries and helping these countries to contain inflation and maintain economic stability. Chinese outbound investments increase local revenue and promote local economic development by creating employment opportunities. In summary, as China's economy expands, it will not only raise global trade volume but also create more global investment opportunities. More importantly, China has become an engine of global economic growth. China's economy will continue to grow, as her modernization mission has not yet been accomplished. China has to continue to work hard and is progressing well on the road to a prosperous, democratic, and harmonious country. China's goal is to "promote friendship and partnership with her neighboring countries and coexist in harmony with all the nations in the world." China will become an important and indispensable force to maintain peace, development, and political stability in the world.

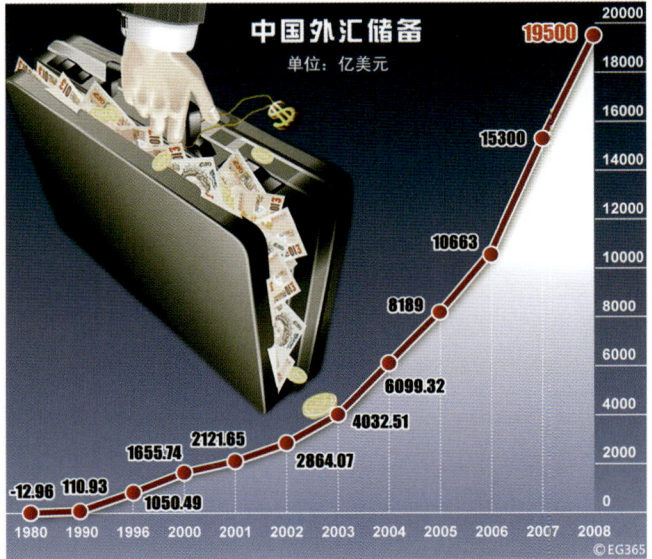

After her entry into the WTO, China has actively participated in international trade activities. China's foreign exchange reserve acts as a financial stabilizer for herself and the world. As of September 2009, the balance of China's foreign exchange reserves was US$2.2726 trillion.

INDEX